New Creative Techniques from a
French Master Chef

translated by kate whiteman   photographed by martin brigdale

new creative techniques from a
French Master Chef

michel **roux**

whitecap

Creative Director: Mary Evans
Publishing Director: Anne Furniss
Project Editors: Janet Illsley and
Carole Clements
Design: Paul Welti
Translator and Editor: Kate Whiteman
Photographer: Martin Brigdale
Stylist: Helen Trent

First published in 2002 by
Quadrille Publishing Limited
Alhambra House
27–31 Charing Cross Road
London WC2H OLS

Published in Canada in 2003 by
Whitecap Books Ltd
For more information, contact
Whitecap Books at 351 Lynn Avenue,
North Vancouver, British Columbia,
Canada, V7J 2C4

ISBN: 1-55285-477-9
Printed and bound in Singapore

dedication

I dedicate this book to the artisans whose produce enables
me to cook the way I do. Without them I would lose my
passion. To ensure that the cycle of quality continues, they
steadfastly refuse to compromise their principles. They
work without counting the hours, and are as dedicated to
their products as I am to the finished result on the plate.
I thank you all.

contents

notes

All spoon and cup measures are level unless otherwise suggested.
Flour is all-purpose, unless otherwise specified, and is spooned into
cup measures and leveled off, not scooped.
Butter is unsalted.
All herbs are fresh unless otherwise suggested.
All eggs are size large unless otherwise stated, and I recommend
you use organic or free-range eggs from a certified and inspected
source. Those in a vulnerable health group, including anyone who
is pregnant, ill, or infirm, should avoid those recipes that contain
raw or lightly cooked egg, which may pose a health risk.
Ovens and broilers must be preheated to the specified temperature.

introduction

How intoxicating it feels to participate in the evolution of cooking for the benefit and happiness of all food lovers! Merely moving with the times can be banal and boring, but my five senses come alive when I am involved in the development of new culinary trends. Thanks to an innate desire to create, mine is a progressive style of cooking, based on the natural flavors and qualities of the products I use. I want to give life back to the ingredients I cook, not to neutralize or stifle them with inappropriate techniques or an excessive use of herbs or spices.

Throughout my long career, while creating new menus at The Waterside Inn, writing numerous books, and educating hundreds of young cooks and *pâtissiers*, professional and non-professional alike, my mantra has always been "modern cuisine, constantly evolving cuisine." Amidst the profusion of gastronomic excesses and tastes of those wannabe culinary stars, some of whom have no real conception of what cooking is about, I can remain serene.

This book reflects my personal aspirations, those of a gourmet who only cooks what he likes to eat. Each chapter guides you through the different cooking methods that have been refined to perfection. The recipes are simple, creative, and sophisticated, and accessible to all my readers.

Martin Brigdale's superb step-by-step photography and pictures of the finished dishes will give you the confidence to recreate these recipes; they truly illustrate the originality and inventiveness of the dishes. It gives me enormous pleasure to share with you my understanding of the ingredients and products that are so valuable in the cooking that I do today.

I am passionate about food. Even cooking a simple bowl of rice can evoke a range of emotional responses, as I take in the different aromas arising from Thai jasmine or sticky rice, basmati, arborio, short, long, or round grain, and wild rice. Cooking rice to perfection demands skill, and this simple task gives me satisfaction.

I love to experience the refined cuisines of my colleagues, particularly Paul Bocuse, Michel Guérard, and Pierre Gagnaire, with their different styles … classical, modern, or eclectic. In their different ways, they all produce something sublime; I adore this, and the emotion it evokes. Cooks are *artistes*; like painters, musicians, sculptors, and singers, they all have their own unique style, one is not better than another; they are simply different.

regional produce

I like to find inspiration in local produce, but sadly, it is fast disappearing. Most of our small farmers no longer have local slaughterhouses where they can send their animals, while producers of vegetables, fruit, cheeses, honey, and the like, cannot continue their struggle against the food giants (although, of course, many still battle for survival).

The flood of European Union regulations and directives seems designed to ensure that everything that could be good and beautiful is brought to its lowest common denominator. Standardization is almost forced, to the detriment of quality. Fruit and vegetables are picked weeks before they reach maturity, and are flown on a round-the-world trip or driven the length and breadth of Europe in refrigerated trucks. It doesn't take much imagination to picture the end result on the consumer's plate.

I must admit, I find it hard to keep my cool when I see how the authorities treat European consumers, who have known better and would love to maintain or even improve the quality of the foods they eat. I do, however, find reassurance in the tide of public opposition to genetically modified foods, which are a danger to the consumer, the environment, and the inhabitants of the countryside.

Personally, I encourage the use of local organic produce in my kitchens at The Waterside Inn; sadly, I can't use them exclusively, because production is on a small scale, but I do use whatever my local producer can provide, even if he only supplies on an occasional basis. Let us hope that good sense will prevail, and that all is not lost! We must continue to fight for what we deserve.

treasures of the sea

The seas, oceans, rivers, and lakes that make up almost 70% of our planet provide a huge reservoir of food. Seaweed, for example, adds new iodized flavors to my cooking. I first discovered laverbread over 20 years ago in Wales. More recently, I have been buying marsh and rock samphire from Rungis market, near Paris, to use as a garnish for fish terrines, or in a *salade gourmande* – my seasonal

"I intend
to promote
completely
unfamiliar
and untried
varieties of
fish, which
will cost
far less"

salad hors d'oeuvre prepared with delicate ingredients fresh from the market. Note that, strictly speaking, samphire is not seaweed, but a marine vegetable.

There are many varieties of edible seaweed, all different in appearance, color, and texture. Some have the flavor of dried mushrooms, others of sorrel, oysters, or smoked tea; some even have a sweet flavor. In my cooking, seaweed is always used judiciously and parsimoniously, in the same way as spices. It is a subtle ingredient, a sort of condiment, which I mainly use in fish dishes, like salmon en papillote with pine needles (page 137), and my seafood crêpes (page 58). It also features in my croustade with vegetable "spaghetti" (page 173).

At present, the seaweeds I use most often are sea lettuce, dulse, laver, wakame, royal and Breton kombu, and sea spaghetti, which are widely available in health food stores. I love their appearance and taste, and the contemporary, healthy quality they impart to my dishes.

I like to prepare and cook fish using simple techniques that bring out the full intrinsic flavor of the prime ingredient. Baking fish in a salt crust (page 134) is an excellent way to seal in the flavors and highlight the natural perfection of the fish. I love to serve this with a contrasting drizzle of chive oil and lemon wedges (illustrated on page 6). The freshest of fish can be served raw, lightly smoked, or cured (see pages 34–7). Freshly caught sea bream, for example, is delicious "cooked" in salt: mix 1 pound coarse salt with 1/4 cup sugar and 1/2 teaspoon crushed peppercorns. Fillet the fish, sprinkle with the salt mixture, wrap in plastic wrap, and refrigerate for about 2 hours. Rinse under a trickle of water, pat dry, then slice thinly like smoked salmon. Arrange the slices on a plate for everyone to help themselves, and add lemon juice and olive oil to taste. Toasted country bread makes the perfect accompaniment to this wonderfully natural "fisherman's dish."

I realize that I am not alone in choosing to eat more produce from the sea, and that, as we consume ever more of it, we risk depleting certain marine species. I want to alert consumers to this danger, and encourage them to discover new, hitherto unknown varieties. Until now, I have tended to use only traditional fish in my recipes. In future, I intend to promote unfamiliar and untried fish that will cost far less than sole, monkfish, or turbot, which are becoming ridiculously expensive owing to an insatiable demand.

lemon: my favorite

How I admire this unique ingredient. Not only is the lemon the epitome of health, bursting with vitamin C, but it is multifaceted, and has so many wonderful and astonishing uses. I adore the bright yellow color, compact shape, and skin (thin-skinned fruit are my preference). The fragrance, acid juice, and extraordinary versatility combine to make the lemon "the king of ingredients" in my eyes. Lemons are my loyal indispensable companions in the kitchen; if they did not exist, I should have to create them, since I use them more than any herb, spice, or condiment.

Lemons are grown in many Mediterranean countries, but my favorites come from Amalfi on the southern Italian coast. Sold complete with stalks and some of their leaves, they have an exceptional aroma and flavor that justify their high price. Every part is edible, and I urge you not to eschew them.

I grate the peel and use it to perfume madeleines and fresh pasta; I pare the zests to decorate desserts, and dry or freeze them to perfume beef daubes and sauces in winter; I candy them to make aiguillettes of candied peel coated in chocolate. My guests adore the lemon marmalade that I love to make as a change from the orange variety. Lemon seeds are rich in pectin and can be used as a setting agent for other jellies and jams, too.

I often put a lemon peel in the switched-off oven after cooking fish to get rid of the smell, or dry slices to add a note of freshness to a potpourri. Even my copper cooking pots enjoy the benefits of lemon; mix the juice with a little fine sand, coarse salt, a few egg whites, and the leftover lemon skin, then rub over copper

to give it a miraculous shine. The only creatures who fear my trusty favorite are ants; a few small pieces of lemon placed along their trail keeps them at bay until I buy a more noxious deterrent!

The acidity of lemon juice accentuates, enlivens, and refines my sauces; even those that aren't asleep are galvanized by the minor whiplash it gives them. It enhances and develops the aromas of fruit coulis and sorbets, like my famous lemon "colonel sorbet" with an added dash of vodka, which is often served at The Waterside Inn. A drizzle of lemon juice squeezed over freshly peeled fruits, like bananas, apples, pears, peaches, and avocados, as well as sliced mushrooms, peeled artichoke hearts, and many other vegetables, will prevent them from oxidizing and turning black on the surface. I also put in a piece of lemon when boiling new potatoes to stop them from bursting.

Lemon juice is sometimes substituted for vinegar in my vinaigrettes, especially for summer salads of tender leaves or thinly sliced mushrooms, and it is used in my marinades for fish to be served raw. A good way to check the freshness of certain shellfish is to squeeze lemon juice onto the flesh; oysters and scallops in particular will contract if they are spanking fresh.

When making caramel, once it has reached the right degree of cooking, I add the juice of a lemon to liquefy it. I store this caramel extract in a bottle to use as a delicious addition to certain desserts, like crème caramel and rice pudding, or instead of sugar to sweeten and flavor whipped cream.

On long winter evenings, I love to sip a piping hot grog made with lemon juice, honey, and a little rum, topped up with boiling water. By contrast, during my military service in North Africa, I used to make a refreshing hot weather drink by adding a few drops of lemon juice, reinforced with a pinch of salt, to a glass of lemonade.

I salt lemons to use in North African chicken and fish dishes by making incisions in the fruit and rubbing in salt crystals. My *pieds-noirs* friends cut salted lemons into quarters and serve them with other canapés as *kemia*, the equivalent of Spanish tapas.

"fragrance,
acid juice, and
extraordinary
versatility
combine to
make the lemon
the king of
ingredients in
my eyes"

And that's not all. Lemon juice has soothing qualities. I remember my mother rubbing it into her elbows to soften the skin. Even now, when I finish preparing and cooking a dish, I never fail to rub my hands with the remains of a lemon, then sniff it to enjoy its scent. I am not the only one who appreciates the lemon. Every year, during February in the village of Menton, close to the Italian border in the South of France, the "festival of the lemon" is held, and the virtues of this prized citrus fruit are celebrated with great gusto.

liquid gold

Year by year, olive oil plays an increasingly important role in my cooking. The moment I arrive in the South of France, I am inspired by the Mediterranean climate to snatch the bottle of liquid gold from the cupboard, pour a drizzle onto a plate, and dunk a piece of fresh crusty bread. Heaven! Throughout my stay, I completely abandon the echiré butter that I use as often as olive oil in a harsher climate.

Olive oil is produced in almost all Mediterranean countries, where it occupies a place of honor and every village boasts that theirs is the best. I enjoy wandering through the local fairs when

olive oils are the main attraction, tasting and comparing. I love them all, although each one is different. Their colors range from greenish-yellow to olive green; each has its unique savor and aroma, density, or lightness.

I use the lightest oils for cooking dishes like pan-fried monkfish with red pepper confit (page 142), and reserve the punchier, fruity varieties for marinades for fish that will be served raw. I use it abundantly in my *sauce vierge* and *rouille* for my bouillabaisse; substitute it for cream in a potato purée; preserve tomatoes, peppers, and garlic in it (see pages 79–80); drizzle it over delicious tiny red mullet or sea bream in a fine salt crust (page 134), and add a slug to fresh pasta with a few basil leaves. And so on …

Olive oil adds vitality to my cooking, making it more digestible and modern. I never fail to buy a couple of flagons when I find a new producer in a far-flung place; after all, olive trees are not exclusive to the Mediterranean, but grow in other continents. California, Australia, and South Africa all produce fine olive oils. One of my favorites, Morgenster, is produced by Giulio Bertrand near Capetown.

I enjoy sharing, discovering, discussing, and even arguing about its merits with my colleagues. Like *grands crus* bordeaux wines, the price escalates according to whether it is virgin, first pressing, extra virgin, or even classified as AOC (*appellation contrôlée*). The label of these fine oils is often festooned with gold medals that have been won in fiercely contested competitions.

And finally, it has remedial qualities. When visiting a wine-producing region, I swallow a couple of spoonfuls of neat olive oil before embarking on a lengthy wine-tasting session. It lines and soothes my stomach, preventing the heartburn and acidity which are always a possible consequence of these protracted tastings, which can sometimes extend over two or three days …

As you may have gathered, I am passionate about olive oil – quite an admission for the son of a mother from Normandy, where butter is extolled as king.

culinary equipment

I insist that all my kitchen equipment and utensils are efficient and durable – qualities that are reflected in their price. I only buy the very best ingredients, so my cooking and *pâtisserie* equipment must be of equally high quality to ensure that my dishes are cooked to perfection. Rather than list a hundred items to equip your kitchen, I prefer to tell you about a few of my favorites. You will find a list of suppliers on page 189.

I am still using many of the knives that I have had since my apprenticeship; some of the Sabatier knives are still in good condition and their blades, which I sharpen regularly, never let me down. For the past ten years, I have favored Japanese Global knives, which give incomparable high-precision results. There are over fifty different types, each designed for a specific use, but many can be put to multiple use. To provide a collection to last a lifetime, I recommend that you choose five or ten of the following knives: 10-inch Yanagi sashimi, vegetable, carving, serrated, ham, salmon, filleting, boning, paring, utility. You will also need a sharpener to keep them razor-sharp; I recommend the Global ceramic whetstone for domestic use.

The old cast-iron frying pans our grandmothers used are hard to find nowadays, and sadly not such good quality, so I have made the decision to use nonstick pans. After experimenting with many brands, I now use Tefal in my kitchens at home and at The Waterside Inn. The surface of these durable pans does not scratch easily, and there is a wide choice of shapes and sizes. My omelets, crêpes, and blinis have never been better.

For making stock, I use enormous tinned copper stockpots, which I have had for thirty years. Unfortunately, they need re-tinning every three to six months, and it is very hard to find anyone to perform this onerous task nowadays – another example of a fast-disappearing craft. Gradually, I am replacing these pots with stainless steel stockpots or deep saucepans, with reinforced bases that ensure even heat distribution.

All my shallow vegetable pans, deep sauté pans for meat, and small pans for sauces, are made from materials that can withstand fierce heat and cook evenly. They must be strong enough to stand up to daily use by a brigade of twenty chefs. I have chosen the American All-Clad brand, which can cope with occasional ill-treatment, and lasts for at least ten years in a professional kitchen – the equivalent of a lifetime in a domestic environment!

Some years ago, Paul Bocuse introduced me to the Staub brand from Alsace. I use their cast-iron casseroles and the small gratin dishes in which I cook eggahs and the like. Staub also make a self-simmering pan, which uses an ingenious system of evaporation, condensation, and spraying that guarantees perfect cooking results.

For twenty years, I have used a Braun hand blender to aerate my sauces, *nages,* and bouillons, to make them light and frothy. I use this quality blender every day for pastry, fish, and meat dishes and soups, and couldn't live without it.

My collection of small implements includes a little marvel of an asparagus peeler made by Monopol in Germany, which I discovered on a farm in northern France where the grower sold asparagus directly to the public. As you peel the asparagus, it follows the contours of the stalks, making it impossible to break them ... a remarkable gadget.

A compact, battery-operated kitchen scale is essential. It weighs very precisely, which is useful for spices and yeast, as well as flour, vegetables, and other ingredients. Cooking thermometers are also important, notably oven, sugar, and meat thermometers (essential for checking internal temperature). Since no built-in gauge accurately indicates the true temperature inside an oven, I regard an oven thermometer as indispensable when cooking fragile confections like macaroons, choux puffs, and meringues.

I could carry on extolling the merits of many other utensils, gadgets, and equipment. While others might browse around antique stores, I love to visit the specialist cookshop, Mora, in Paris. It's like Aladdin's cave, and I spend hours there, filling my suitcases with whisks, cutters, spatulas, and so on ... I recommend a visit.

marinades, stocks, and sauces

This chapter is the stairway to cooking. Each of the three elements it features will add a new dimension to your dishes, bringing them to life in an unexpected and magical way.

The purpose of a marinade is to develop and enhance the flavors of an ingredient, not to neutralize them. Excessive use of herbs, spices, lemon, vinegar, soy sauce, tamarind, ginger, and other aromatics will suffocate and dry meats, fish, and seafood. Thin slices of fish or shellfish need only about 10 minutes' marinating to benefit

from the process, and should not drown in the flavors of the marinade, however well balanced it may be. I use a sweetened marinade with a touch of spice for dishes like my marinated mackerel diamonds (page 38). One useful tip: a little papaya juice applied to tough meat will help to tenderize it in 10 to 15 minutes.

Stocks have long been the foundation stone of cooking. In recent years, mine have become lighter and I use them in moderation. I like to prepare shellfish-based *nages*, which I sometimes serve cold, with a few tender, tasty seasonal vegetables and shreds of blanched seaweed. I often clarify these *nages* with lobster or langoustine flesh – somewhat extravagant, but worth it for the incomparably elegant end result.

On a practical note, stocks should always be cooled quickly to prevent bacteria developing. Use a bowl set over ice, or a blast chiller in a professional kitchen.

Sauces are the cook's alchemy; a little magic potion, a few herbs and spices, and the sauce is under way. They are the backroom boys who underpin, stabilize, and accompany a dish, but they play a vital role. Sauces enhance the flavors of ingredients with vigor and panache; a carefully prepared, harmonious sauce will meld into a dish and become an integral part.

I love all sauces – hot, cold, with a hint of wine, sweet-sour, or even quite plain. I like them to be expressive, with a lingering finish, light, ephemeral as a butterfly. I create them as the fancy takes me, according to my mood, my appetite, to satisfy my palate, to be the perfect partner for the food they accompany.

The best way to reheat sauces is in a *bain-marie*, or water bath. You can use a microwave, but be careful with the timing. Some sauces, like hollandaise and other emulsions cannot be kept waiting, so prepare them just before you serve them.

As for vinaigrettes and salsas, I mainly use these in my spring and summer dishes. I vary the colors, textures, and liveliness according to the salads, crudités, shellfish, terrines, pasta, and rice dishes they accompany. They are quick to prepare and you can add a fruity note with mango, pineapple, raspberries, and pears. Let your imagination run riot, but use your common sense. When using shallots in a salsa, I tone down the harshness by chopping them finely and rinsing them in a sieve under a trickle of cold water.

Fruit coulis enhance many of my desserts, but I only use very ripe, seasonal fruits. My gingered pear coulis (page 28), for example, will be full of flavor and nuances if it is made with very ripe pears.

cooked marinade for meat and game

The main purpose of a marinade is to infuse the meat with flavor, and to make the texture a little softer. A small quantity of marinade added to a game sauce, or used to deglaze a roasting pan, will delicately perfume the sauce or *jus*.

Always use a fork or tongs when handling meat in a marinade. Never use your fingers to put it in, take it out, or turn it, as this could ruin the marinade, turning it sour and making it unusable.

Put the meat in a nonmetal container large enough to hold it and enough marinade to cover it generously. The amount of marinade you will need and the marinating time is determined by the size of each piece. For example, a leg of lamb will need about 12 hours in the marinade, while a fillet of venison will need only 2 to 3 hours.

Makes 1½ quarts

2 tablespoons butter
3 medium carrots, peeled and cut into rounds
³/4 cup coarsely chopped onions
2 celery stalks, thinly sliced
4 cups red wine, preferably Côtes du Rhône
6 tablespoons red wine vinegar
3 cups water
1 large bouquet garni, including a sprig of rosemary
1 small head of garlic (unpeeled), halved widthwise
¹/4 ounce mace blades, or a pinch ground mace
2 cloves
¹/2 teaspoon crushed peppercorns

Melt the butter in a saucepan over a low heat. Add the vegetables and sweat gently for 5 minutes. Add all the other ingredients, bring to a boil over a high heat, then lower the heat and cook gently for 20 minutes, skimming the surface as necessary.

Let cool, then strain the marinade through a fine conical sieve and refrigerate until ready to use.

quick meat marinade

I use this for broiled or pan-fried dishes that use small pieces of meat and poultry – medallions of venison (page 115), beef tournedos, veal fillet, lamb chops, and chicken breasts.

Put the cut meat in a nonmetallic dish, trickle over olive oil to cover, and scatter over some sprigs of thyme and rosemary, a few bay leaves, crushed peppercorns, and sliced garlic. Turn the meat over in the marinade so that it is impregnated all over. Cover the dish with plastic wrap and let marinate for at least 1 hour.

When ready to cook, dab off the excess oil, herbs, and spices. Salt the meat only just before cooking.

quick fish marinade

Combine olive oil and lemon juice (ratio of 5 to1) with a few delicate herb leaves, like basil. Put the prepared fish in a nonmetallic dish and cover with the marinade. Turn the fish over to impregnate it all over. Cover with plastic wrap. Marinate small pieces of fish for about 30 minutes; allow up to an hour for larger pieces.

Just before cooking the fish, dab off the excess oil, herbs, and spices. Salt the fish only just before cooking.

sweet-sour marinade

This is ideal for oily fish; I use it for my marinated mackerel diamonds (page 38), illustrated opposite.

Serves 6

1²/3 cups water
¹/2 cup sugar
¹/2 cup lemon juice
2 small black licorice sticks (twigs), lightly crushed
4 star anise

Combine the water, sugar, and lemon juice in a saucepan and bring to a boil. Toss in the licorice sticks and star anise and simmer for 1 minute.

chicken stock

This is used in many sauces and to enrich *jus*, but it can be served as a bouillon in its own right, with a few tarragon leaves or some lemon grass added.

Makes about 1½ quarts

1 stewing chicken, about 3¹/₄ pounds, or the equivalent weight of chicken carcasses, wings, or thighs, blanched and refreshed
2¹/₂ quarts cold water
2 large carrots, cut into rounds
white part of 2 leeks, thinly sliced
1 onion, peeled and studded with 2 cloves
2 cups thinly sliced button mushrooms
1 large bouquet garni (to include celery)
1 teaspoon crushed peppercorns

Put the chicken in a saucepan, add the water, and bring to a boil over a high heat. Immediately lower the heat and simmer gently for 10 minutes, skimming as necessary. Add all the other ingredients. Cook gently, allowing 1¹/₂ hours for a whole bird or about 50 minutes for pieces or carcasses; skim regularly.

Strain the stock through a fine conical sieve into a bowl and cool quickly over ice. Refrigerate for up to 5 days.

fish stock

Makes about 2 quarts

3¹/₄ pounds bones and/or trimmings of sole, turbot, brill, or whiting, cut into pieces
3 tablespoons butter
¹/₂ cup thinly sliced onions
white parts of 2 leeks, thinly sliced
1 cup thinly sliced button mushrooms
³/₄ cup dry white wine
2¹/₂ quarts cold water
1 bouquet garni
2 lemon slices
8 white peppercorns, coarsely crushed, and tied in cheesecloth

Rinse the fish bones and trimmings under cold running water to remove any blood, and drain.

Melt the butter in a saucepan, add the vegetables, and sweat over a low heat for a few minutes. Add the fish bones and trimmings, simmer gently for a few minutes, then add the wine, and reduce by two-thirds.

Pour in the water, bring to a boil, then lower the heat to a very gentle simmer, and skim. Add the bouquet garni and lemon slices. Simmer gently for 15 minutes, skimming as necessary. Add the peppercorns and simmer for another 10 minutes. Gently ladle the stock through a fine conical sieve into a bowl and cool over ice, as quickly as possible.

vegetable stock

The vegetables can be varied according to your taste and the season – ripe tomatoes in summer, woodland mushrooms (especially chanterelles) in the fall, and so on. To make a *nage*, which is a light poaching liquid rather than a classic stock, I add a touch of acidity – in this case vinegar.

Makes about 2 quarts
3 large carrots, peeled and cut into rounds
white parts of 2 leeks, thinly sliced
2 celery stalks, thinly sliced
1/2 cup very thinly sliced bulb fennel
1 1/4 cups thinly sliced shallots
2/3 cup peeled and thinly sliced onion
2 unpeeled garlic cloves
1 bouquet garni
1 cup dry white wine
2 quarts water
10 white peppercorns, coarsely crushed, and tied in cheesecloth
3 tablespoons white wine vinegar (only for a nage)

Put all the ingredients in a saucepan. Bring to a boil over a high heat, then lower the heat and simmer gently for 45 minutes, skimming the surface as necessary. Strain through a fine conical sieve into a bowl and cool over ice, as quickly as possible.

lemon and mint vinaigrette

This refreshing vinaigrette is the perfect foil for watercress and it features in my poached eggs on watercress salad with red pepper salsa (page 54). It also makes an excellent dressing for grated carrot or a warm salad of cooked cauliflower.

Serves 6
2 lemons
6 mint leaves
6 tablespoons peanut oil
salt and freshly ground pepper

Wash and dry the lemons, finely grate the zest of one, and squeeze the juice of both of them. Roll up the mint leaves and finely snip them.

Put the lemon zest and juice in a bowl with the oil, season with salt and pepper, and whisk to mix. Stir in the mint at the very last moment, just before serving.

sherry vinaigrette

This is a superb dressing for crisp salad leaves, like Belgian endive, chicory or dandelion, or for French beans or potatoes that are served warm.

Serves 6
2 eggs
3 tablespoons sherry vinegar
6 tablespoons peanut oil
2 thin strips bacon, fried until crisp and finely crumbled
salt and freshly ground pepper

Add the eggs to a pan of boiling water and hard-boil for no longer than 6 minutes. Cool quickly in cold water, then shell and finely chop the eggs, or work them through a sieve. Put them in a bowl and season with salt and pepper. Whisk in the vinegar, then the peanut oil. Finally, add the bacon.

sauce suprême

I sometimes enrich this sauce with egg yolks, particularly if it is to be glazed under the broiler. Poached oysters, lightly coated with sauce suprême and glazed under the broiler until warm, are divine. I also use the sauce in my seafood crêpes (page 58), illustrated opposite. If you are serving sauce suprême on its own, it will be less rich without the egg yolks.

Makes 1 quart

1 quart velouté sauce (see left)
6 tablespoons heavy cream
2 egg yolks (optional)
2 small pinches of saffron threads (optional)
salt and freshly ground pepper

In a saucepan, gently heat the velouté sauce, stirring occasionally with a whisk. As soon as it comes to a boil, add the cream, and the egg yolks, if using. Allow the sauce to bubble for only 2 minutes if you are using egg yolks, or 5 minutes if not.

Season with salt and pepper to taste, and add the saffron, if using, rubbing the threads between your fingertips. Whisk and heat gently until simmering.

velouté sauce

This velvety sauce can be served as it is, but it's also used as the base for sauce suprême (see right) and, in smaller quantities, for other white sauces. The addition of a spoonful or two of velouté will add body to a white wine sauce to accompany fish. It is important to note that if the white roux is hot, the added stock must be cold, and vice-versa, otherwise the sauce will be lumpy.

Makes 1 quart

3 tablespoons butter
1/4 cup flour, sifted
1 quart fish stock (page 16), chicken stock (page 16), or vegetable stock (page 17)
salt and freshly ground pepper

First make a white roux. Melt the butter in a heavy-based saucepan. Off the heat, add the flour and stir it in with a whisk. Return to a medium heat and cook for 3 minutes, stirring continuously.

Pour the cold stock onto the roux, stirring all the time, then cook the sauce over a low heat for about 30 minutes, stirring occasionally with a whisk. Season with salt and pepper to taste.

hollandaise sauce

This light, classic sauce is delicate and should be served as soon as it is made, though you can keep it warm for 10 to 15 minutes. I serve it with grilled lobster with garden herbs (page 119), and my salmon mousse and spinach tartlets (page 70).

Hollandaise is the inspiration for other sauces. For a noisette sauce to serve with fish, whisk 3 tablespoons browned butter at room temperature into hollandaise just before serving.

Serves 6

1 tablespoon white wine vinegar
4 tablespoons cold water
1 teaspoon white peppercorns, crushed
4 egg yolks
1/2 pound butter, clarified (page 188), cooled to tepid
juice of 1/2 lemon
salt

Put the vinegar, water, and pepper in a small pan, set on a low heat and reduce by one-third. Leave until cold.

Add the egg yolks and mix with a whisk. Stand the pan on a heat diffuser over a very low heat and continue to whisk, keeping the whisk in contact with the base of the pan. Still whisking continuously, very gradually increase the heat to no more than 150°F, so that the sauce emulsifies extremely slowly; it will take 8 to 10 minutes to become smooth and creamy.

Off the heat, trickle in the tepid butter, whisking as you go. Season with salt. Stir in the lemon juice at the last moment. Serve at once.

curry mayonnaise

This versatile mayonnaise goes well with crudités, vegetable tempura (page 152), hard-boiled eggs, cold roast chicken, and any cold poached firm-fleshed white fish. You can lighten it by folding in 1/4 to 1/2 cup plain yogurt, or make it creamier by adding 2 tablespoons crème fraîche or sour cream.

For an original twist on plain mayonnaise, omit the curry powder and add 2 or 3 spoonfuls of reduced tomato coulis. For a mustardy mayonnaise, replace the curry powder with a generous pinch of English mustard powder.

Makes about 1¼ cups

1 tablespoon strong Dijon mustard
2 egg yolks, at room temperature
1 cup peanut oil, at room temperature
1 tablespoon curry powder (mild or hot, to taste)
2 tablespoons lemon juice, or warm wine vinegar
salt and freshly ground pepper

Combine the mustard, salt, and pepper in a bowl. Add the egg yolks and immediately mix these ingredients together with a small whisk.

Whisk in the oil, drop by drop to begin with, then in a thin stream, until it is all incorporated.

Dissolve the curry powder in the lemon juice or vinegar, and stir it into the mayonnaise. Taste and add more salt and pepper, if necessary. Whisk for another 30 seconds to make a thick, glossy mayonnaise.

Serve immediately, or cover with plastic wrap and refrigerate the mayonnaise for up to 3 hours.

red pepper salsa

I like to serve this salsa with my ham mousse (page 69), but it is equally delicious eaten alone, spread on toast. I prefer to char the peppers on a charcoal grill (to which I add some vine shoots). If this isn't convenient, blister the skins in a hot oven or under a very hot broiler, though the flavor won't be quite as good. If the peppers are not as sweet as they should be, add some chopped confit tomatoes (page 79).

Serves 8

4 red sweet Italian or bell peppers
2 small yellow bell peppers (optional)
1/2 cup olive oil
2 shallots, peeled and finely chopped
leaves from 2 small thyme sprigs, chopped
10 to 12 basil leaves, snipped
juice of 2 lemons
salt and freshly ground pepper

Using your fingertips, oil the peppers very lightly. Broil them, or, preferably, grill them until the skins are blistered and blackened.

Plunge the peppers into a bowl of water filled with ice cubes, then take out and peel off the skin.

Halve the peppers, remove the core, and scrape out the white membranes and seeds. Cut the peppers into long thin strips. If you are using yellow peppers, cut them into julienne and set aside to add a final touch of color to the salsa.

Dice the red peppers as finely as possible and place in a bowl. The texture should be almost pulpy – halfway between tiny dice and a coulis.

Add the shallots, thyme and basil to the red peppers, season with salt and pepper, and stir in the olive oil and lemon juice. Mix carefully, adding the yellow pepper julienne if using.

Serve the salsa immediately, or cover with plastic wrap and keep in the refrigerator for up to 48 hours.

pear and lime salsa

This makes a delicious accompaniment to my wild boar and morel pâté en croûte (page 73) and all meat-based terrines. It is also good served cold with my terrine of baby vegetables (page 77). The salsa keeps well in the fridge for a week.

Serves 8

Poaching liquid:

2 cups water
1 cup sugar
juice of 1/2 lemon

Salsa:

2 very ripe pears
1/4 cup finely chopped shallots
2 to 3 cornichons or small gherkins, cut into thin strips
grated zest of 1/2 lime
juice of 1/2 lime
3 tablespoons olive oil
4 very ripe raspberries
salt and freshly ground pepper

Combine the water, sugar, and lemon juice in a saucepan. Peel the pears, halve lengthwise, and remove the cores. Add them to the poaching liquid and bring to a boil. Immediately lower the heat and poach the pears gently until lightly cooked; this will take about 10 minutes, depending how ripe they are. Allow to cool completely in the syrup.

Drain the pears, cut into small dice, and place in a bowl. Add the other ingredients, lightly crushing the raspberries with a fork. Season with pepper to taste and add just a pinch of salt.

herb salsa

This salsa goes particularly well with my wild mushroom cappelletti (page 88). You can also serve it with steamed cauliflower or green beans as an hors d'oeuvre, or with grilled tuna.

Serves 6

1 very small potato, about 2 ounces
1¹/4 cups snipped fines herbes *(tarragon, chervil, and flat-leaf parsley)*
2¹/2 tablespoons sherry vinegar
¹/2 cup olive oil
juice of 1 lemon
5 tablespoons finely chopped scallions
1 tablespoon coarse grain mustard (e.g., Meaux)
salt and freshly ground pepper

Boil the potato in its skin, then peel, and press through the coarse blade of a vegetable mill or potato ricer.

Combine all the ingredients in a bowl, mix well, and season with salt and pepper to taste.

green olive and lemon salsa

This is an excellent accompaniment to my tartares of salmon and scallops in endive leaves (page 40), most cold poached fish and vegetable crudités.

Serves 6

1 small potato, about 2³/4 ounces
1 lemon
juice of 2 lemons
12 green olives, pitted and finely diced
1 tablespoon snipped flat-leaf parsley
pinch of saffron threads, infused in 1 tablespoon warm water
6 tablespoons olive oil
5 tablespoons finely chopped scallions
salt and freshly ground pepper

Boil the potato in its skin, then peel it, and press through the coarse blade of a vegetable mill or potato ricer. Peel the lemon, cutting off all pith and membrane, then cut it into segments.

Combine all the ingredients in a bowl, mix well, and season with salt and pepper to taste.

sweet and sour sauce

I like to serve this unusual sauce with langoustine and squid tempura (page 153) and my sashimi (page 37), but it is good with ham and other cold meat dishes too. Veal stock gives a rich depth of flavor, but you can use chicken stock (page 16) or vegetable stock (page 17) and reduce the sauce for longer to intensify the taste.

Stored in an airtight jar in the fridge, sweet and sour sauce will keep well for 2 weeks.

Makes about ¾ cup

7 ounces (about 2 small) green bell peppers
7 ounces (about 2 small) red bell peppers
2 tablespoons peanut oil
1¹/4 cups finely chopped onions
¹/2 cup Demerara or light brown sugar
6 tablespoons red wine vinegar
²/3 cup veal stock (homemade or bought)

Peel the peppers as for red pepper salsa (page 22). Halve, core, and seed them, then dice.

Gently heat the oil in a heavy-based saucepan. Add the onions and sweat for 5 minutes, stirring with a wooden spoon. Add the peppers and sweat, stirring, for another 5 minutes. Add the sugar and cook until the vegetables are lightly caramelized, stirring all the time.

Pour in the vinegar and deglaze the pan. When the liquid comes to a boil, reduce it by two-thirds over a medium heat. Add the veal stock and cook until the sauce is reduced and lightly coats the back of a spoon. Serve the sauce tepid or cold.

pesto

Flavored with basil, pesto is highly aromatic and widely used in Mediterranean cooking to enhance soups, steamed fish, and pasta. It keeps well for several days in an airtight container in the fridge. Leave it at room temperature for 30 minutes before serving for optimum flavor.

For a denser, richer pesto, add 3 tablespoons toasted pine nuts and pulverize them with the basil. This version is delicious stirred into a risotto or tossed with pasta.

Serves 6

2 garlic cloves, peeled
20 basil leaves
3 1/2 ounces Parmesan cheese, freshly grated
2/3 cup olive oil
salt and freshly ground pepper

Remove the green germ from the middle of each garlic clove. Put the garlic in a mortar, add a pinch of salt and pound to a paste. Add the basil leaves and pound until very smooth.

Add the Parmesan, then trickle in the olive oil, stirring constantly. Season with salt and pepper.

cèpe coulis

This is excellent with poached or pan-fried poultry, or used as a dressing for pasta. Or you can pan-fry cèpes with a touch of garlic and parsley until crunchy, and serve them on a little cèpe coulis as a starter. The contrast of flavors and textures is superb.

Serves 6

6 tablespoons butter
1/4 cup finely chopped shallot
10 ounces fresh cèpes, cleaned (or frozen cèpes, thawed), thinly sliced
1 1/4 cups chicken stock (page 16)
1 small garlic clove, peeled and crushed
1/3 cup snipped flat-leaf parsley
salt and freshly ground pepper

Melt 4 tablespoons of the butter in a saucepan. Add the shallot, then the cèpes, and sweat over a low heat for 5 minutes. Add the stock, garlic, and parsley and cook over a medium heat for 10 minutes.

Tip into a blender and blend for 5 minutes until very smooth, then strain through a conical sieve.

Just before serving, reheat the coulis. Dice the remaining butter and whisk into the coulis at the last minute; season with salt and pepper, and serve.

cucumber coulis

This refreshing coulis goes very well with cold poached fish, smoked salmon, cold omelets, and pasta salads. It will keep for up to 48 hours in the fridge, but the water in the cucumber will cause it to separate, so stir with a small whisk for a few moments just before serving.

Serves 6

1 medium cucumber
1 small red chili
4 to 5 parsley sprigs
6 sage leaves
3 tablespoons olive oil
squeeze of lemon juice, to taste
salt and freshly ground pepper

Peel the cucumber, cut it in half lengthwise, and remove the seeds. Cut the cucumber into chunks and put in a blender.

Halve the chili lengthwise. Scrape out the white membrane and seeds with a small knife, then chop as finely as possible. Add the chili to the blender. (Remember to wash your hands afterwards.)

Whizz the cucumber chunks and chili for 1 minute until fairly smooth. Season with salt and pepper.

Coarsely chop the parsley and sage leaves. Tip them into the blender and process for another minute.

Pour the olive oil into the blender and add a generous squeeze of lemon juice. Blend for about 2 minutes, until smooth and almost creamy. Pour into a bowl. Taste and adjust the seasoning, adding more lemon juice if needed. Cover and refrigerate the coulis until ready to serve.

leek coulis with saffron and dill

This is one of my favorite coulis. It marries well with firm-fleshed fish like brill, monkfish, and turbot, or seafood such as langoustine tails and scallops. As with all savory coulis, you can use vegetable stock rather than chicken stock to satisfy vegetarians.

Serves 6

1 pound young leeks, greenest parts removed
3 tablespoons butter
1¼ cups chicken stock (page 16) or vegetable stock (page 17)
2 small pinches of saffron strands
1¼ cups heavy cream
1 tablespoon chopped dill
salt and freshly ground pepper

Halve the leeks lengthwise, wash thoroughly in cold water, and slice them finely. Blanch in boiling water for 2 minutes, then refresh in cold water and drain well, pressing the leeks to extract all moisture.

Melt the butter in a saucepan, add the leeks, and sweat them gently for 10 minutes. Add the stock, then the saffron, and cook over a medium heat for barely 10 minutes. Add the cream and bubble for 5 minutes.

Tip into a blender and whizz for 2 minutes. Strain through a conical sieve and season with salt and pepper.

Keep the coulis warm if it is to be served soon; otherwise reheat it gently just before serving. Stir in the dill at the very last moment.

saffron mango coulis

Serves 6

2 cups cubed mango flesh
juice of 1 lemon
1 cup sugar syrup (page 188)
pinch of saffron threads

Purée the mango in a blender with the lemon juice and half of the sugar syrup, then pass through a fine sieve.

Heat the remaining sugar syrup in a small saucepan, add the saffron threads, and bring to a boil. Take off the heat and leave to cool. When cold, whisk the syrup into the mango coulis. Cover and refrigerate until needed.

gingered pear coulis

Serves 6

3 very ripe pears, about 7 ounces each
2/3 cup water
3/4 cup sugar
juice of 1/2 lemon
1 tablespoon finely chopped fresh ginger

Peel and core the pears, and cut into pieces. Place in a saucepan with the water, sugar, and lemon juice, and bring to a boil. Lower the heat and poach the pears for 5 to 10 minutes, depending on their ripeness. Add the ginger and cook for 1 to 2 minutes, then leave to cool.

Blitz the cold pear mixture in a blender for 1 minute, then pass through a fine sieve into a bowl; refrigerate until ready to use. If the coulis seems too thick, dilute it with a few spoons of cold water or, better still, port.

red currant and passion fruit coulis

Confectioners' sugar gives this coulis a brilliance which you cannot achieve with granulated sugar. I love to include passion fruit seeds, which float attractively in the clear liquid coulis.

Serves 4 to 6

1/2 pound red currants
1 1/4 to 1 1/2 cups confectioners' sugar, sifted
1 passion fruit, halved

Run the prongs of a fork down the central stem to strip the red currants from their stalks.

Put the red currants into a blender or food processor and whizz for 2 minutes.

Tip the red currant purée into a cheesecloth-lined sieve over a bowl to strain the juice.

When most of the red currant juice has passed through, gather two corners of the cheesecloth in each hand, and twist in opposite directions to extract the remaining juice.

Gradually whisk in the confectioners' sugar – keep tasting the coulis as you add it – the amount you need will depend on the ripeness of the red currants.

Pour the red currant coulis onto the serving plate. Scoop out the passion fruit seeds and pulp and scatter them over the coulis.

coffee sabayon with cinnamon

This sabayon is really a dessert in itself, but it also makes a tempting sauce to serve with fresh orange segments or poached pears (drained of their syrup). I like to serve it simply with lacy orange tuiles – they provide a perfect contrast to the creaminess and fragrance of the sabayon. The hint of cinnamon adds a spicy note and enhances the aroma of the coffee.

Serves 4

1 tablespoon instant coffee granules
$1/4$ cup cold water
4 egg yolks
$1/4$ cup sugar
$1/2$ teaspoon ground cinnamon

To serve (optional):

orange tuiles (page 185)

For your *bain-marie*, half-fill a saucepan that is large enough to hold a round-bottomed copper bowl or pan (or a heatproof glass bowl) with warm water. Place the saucepan over a low heat.

Put the instant coffee and cold water in the bowl and whisk with a balloon whisk to dissolve. Lightly whisk in the egg yolks, sugar, and cinnamon.

Set the bowl in the *bain-marie* and continue to whisk the mixture without stopping for 10 to 12 minutes. It will thicken and increase dramatically in volume as air is incorporated. The sabayon is ready when it is light, fluffy, and shiny, and thick enough to leave a dense ribbon when the whisk is lifted. The water in the *bain-marie* must not exceed 195°F, or the sabayon will start to coagulate; the temperature of the sabayon itself must not go above 150°F. If necessary, turn off or lower the heat as you whisk.

Serve the sabayon in glasses as soon as it is ready. Accompany with orange tuiles, if you like.

chocolate sauce

The sauce is delicious served with poached pears, vanilla or coffee ice cream, meringues, profiteroles, or a banana tart. A dash of Grand Marnier will enhance it and add a sweet spiritous touch.

Serves 6

$3/4$ cup milk
3 tablespoons heavy cream
3 tablespoons sugar
$1/4$ to $1/2$ teaspoon cardamom seeds, crushed
7 ounces best-quality bittersweet chocolate (minimum 70% cocoa solids), or dark couverture, cut into pieces
4 tablespoons butter, at room temperature

Put the milk, cream, and sugar in a saucepan and bring to a boil, stirring continuously. As soon as the milk begins to boil, put in the cardamom seeds, turn off the heat, cover the pan, and leave to infuse for 5 minutes.

Melt the chocolate in a bowl over a pan of hot water, or in the microwave, stirring until smooth. Strain the milk mixture through a fine conical sieve onto the chocolate, stirring with a whisk.

Whisk in the butter, a small piece at a time, to make the sauce smooth and glossy. It is now ready to serve.

chocolate sauce scented with tobacco

I learned of the affinity between chocolate and tobacco from my friend Michel Rostang, who combines them in one of the *petits fours* he serves in his restaurant in Paris. If the idea of eating tobacco alarms you, remember that its truly harmful agents are not produced until it is lit.

Simply infuse the milk mixture with ¼ ounce top-quality Havana or San Dominican cigar leaves rather than cardamom seeds. If you find the tobacco flavor a little too pungent, a dash of Grand Marnier will help to modify it.

pistachio crème anglaise

This unusual custard sauce – delicately flavored and colored with pistachios – is superb with my poached white peaches (page 107), illustrated opposite, and poached pears in sauternes (page 108). Naturally, you can use other flavorings in place of the pistachios.

For a classic crème anglaise, infuse the milk with a split vanilla bean. Or try infusing it with a bunch of fresh mint, or a 1½-inch piece peeled and finely sliced fresh ginger, or 4 star anise.

Alternatively, flavor the milk with 2 ounces melted bittersweet chocolate, or 2 tablespoons instant coffee. And, of course, you can churn and freeze crème anglaise to make a superb ice cream.

Makes about 3 cups

7 ounces shelled pistachios, skinned, or
2¹/₂ tablespoons pistachio paste
6 egg yolks
¹/₂ cup plus 2 tablespoons sugar
2 cups milk

If using fresh pistachios, soak them in cold water for 24 hours. The following day, drain the pistachios and crush to a paste, using a pestle and mortar.

Put the egg yolks in a bowl and whisk in about one-third of the sugar.

Continue whisking until the mixture becomes pale and has a ribbon consistency.

Put the milk and remaining sugar in a saucepan, stir, and bring to a boil, then pour the boiling milk onto the egg and sugar mixture, whisking continuously.

Pour the mixture back into the saucepan and heat gently, stirring continuously with a wooden spoon, until the custard reaches about 175°F and is thick enough to coat the back of the spoon. When you run a fingertip down the back of the spoon, it should leave a trail in the custard. Immediately take off the heat.

Pour one-third of the custard onto the pistachio paste, stirring continuously with a whisk, then stir this mixture back into the custard in the pan.

Pour the custard into a blender and blend for about 3 minutes, until very smooth.

Pass the custard through a fine conical sieve into a bowl, set the bowl over crushed ice and let cool, stirring occasionally with a wooden spoon to prevent a skin forming. When cold, cover the surface with plastic wrap and refrigerate for up to 48 hours until required.

raw and cured food

I am always fascinated by the extreme freshness of the fish that Japanese chefs use to prepare sashimi. I uphold their maxim that the best method of cooking fish that is so fresh is not to cook it at all. Unfortunately, all too frequently, the fish sold in supermarkets has been frozen; this alters the flavor and texture, a fact which my palate never fails to detect when I eat a plate of sashimi. My fishmonger, who specializes in fish for sashimi, provides me with the freshly caught fish that are often so difficult to obtain.

Salt, lemon, sugar, and pepper reign supreme in this chapter, as they are the essential elements of curing and drying. I also explain two ways of smoking. The first is in my lightly smoked duck breasts (page 44), in which orange zests, star anise, and Demerara sugar infuse the duck with mellow, sweet, and spicy aromas. In the second method, I smoke a sea bass fillet (page 47), using a little sawdust – oak, beech, or chestnut, according to taste. I love to smoke certain foods in this way, but only very lightly so that the taste of wood is not discernible. Sadly, commercially smoked foods, like duck and chicken, are often over-smoked in order to disguise their inferior flavor. The same principle applies in wine-making; there is no need to over-oak a fine wine…

For cooking without heat, I use the Tahitian method, applying it to raw fish tartares, like my tartares of salmon and scallops (page 40), scallops marinated in lemon-scented olive olive oil (page 39), and a carpaccio of shellfish. You need an acid ingredient to do the "cooking;" I most often use lemon juice, but occasionally choose a little fresh tomato juice or a few drops of fresh pineapple juice. I might even use a top quality, delicate vinegar such as raspberry, full of the aromas of red berries, or in winter, a cider vinegar redolent of apples. If the flavor demands, I sometimes add a teaspoon of clear lavender honey or maple syrup, which imparts subtle, simply divine flavors.

I regard olive oil as the diva of flavorings. I prefer first pressing extra-virgin olive oil, and use it sparingly to avoid drowning the taste of the main ingredient. Use it plain, or flavored with a few chives (page 188), basil, perhaps even lemon verbena.

Tartares and carpaccios prepared *à la tahitienne* must be served at once to preserve all their flavors. If they are prepared too long in advance, the flavors dissipate. I often serve mini dishes of these fish and shellfish as *amuse-bouches* "compliments of the chef." The delicate taste of the half-cooked seafood sharpens the appetite before a meal.

The technique of curing with salt, with its preservative and antibacterial qualities, dates from the dawn of time. I prefer the dry-salting method, which I apply for only a short time. It draws a natural brine to the surface of the food, which must be rinsed with cold water and patted dry before serving as it is, or cooking.

To finish, I repeat: give your imagination free reign, but don't forget one vital point. Whatever kind of fish, seafood, or meat you intend to salt, cure, or smoke, it must be as fresh as can be. Not only will it taste much better, but think of the risks you run if it is not absolutely spanking fresh…

michel's sashimi

I think of sashimi as a kind of modern meat fondue, in which everyone dips the pieces of fish into the sauce of their choice; the only difference being that the fish for sashimi is eaten raw, while the meat for a fondue is cooked in oil or broth.

As with all sashimi and sushi, the fish and scallops must be of the freshest and finest quality, and it is essential to keep them in the coldest part of the fridge before slicing. For this, you need a knife with a thin, extremely sharp blade or, better still, a special sashimi or sushi knife.

The carrots, daikon, and ginger act as palate-cleansers between bites of each variety of fish dipped into the different sauces. I hope my Japanese colleagues will forgive me this fantasy.

Serves 4

3¹/₂ ounces daikon (white radish)
1 large or 2 small carrots
5 ounces salmon fillet, skinned
5 ounces red tuna or bonito fillet, skinned
5 ounces albacore tuna, skinned
1 sea bream fillet, skinned if preferred
2 mackerel fillets
2 large sea scallops
2 small onions, preferably red, peeled
1 lime

Condiments:

wasabi
soy sauce
extra-virgin olive oil
pickled ginger
sweet and sour sauce (page 24)
sea salt flakes
cracked pepper

Chill 4 serving plates in the fridge. Peel the daikon and carrots and cut into very thin strips, using a mandoline if possible. Place in separate bowls of cold water with some ice cubes.

Cut the salmon and tuna into thin slices, about ¼ inch thick. Slice the bream, mackerel, and the scallops as thinly as possible – the slices should not be more than ¹/₁₆ inch thick.

Slice the onions into thin rings. Slice the lime, then quarter each slice.

To serve, arrange 3 or 4 slices of each kind of fish and some scallop slices elegantly on each chilled plate. Add little piles of daikon and carrot strips, the lime, and a few onion rings. Finally, add the different condiments. Serve immediately, or cover with plastic wrap and refrigerate for no more than a few minutes before serving.

gravlax of halibut

While cruising in Alaska, I developed this idea for curing halibut – in a similar way to the ubiquitous salmon gravlax. It tastes superb, especially with my pear and lime salsa (page 23), and a warm potato salad peppered with watercress leaves. The halibut will keep for a week in the fridge, provided you slice it only just before serving.

Serves 8

1 very fresh halibut fillet on the skin (preferably the dark skin, as the fillets are thicker), about 2 pounds

1 cup fine sea salt

1 cup sugar

3 tablespoons white peppercorns, finely crushed

1/4 cup strong Dijon mustard

2 cups fresh dill, finely chopped, plus 1/2 cup to garnish

3 tablespoons Cognac

2 lemons, quartered, to garnish

Make sure that there are no small bones left in the halibut fillet. Rinse the fish in cold water and pat dry. Make 4 evenly spaced, small diagonal incisions across the middle two-thirds of the fillet on the skin side; the incisions in the thickest part should be deeper.

Mix the salt with the sugar. Put some of this mixture into each incision, with a little crushed pepper, and press lightly with your thumb. Brush each incision with a little mustard, and press on a little chopped dill.

Turn the halibut fillet over, sprinkle with the rest of the pepper, and press firmly to make it adhere. Brush the whole surface with the remaining mustard, sprinkle with the dill, and moisten with the Cognac.

Scatter the remaining salt and sugar mixture generously over the halibut, putting a greater concentration on the thickest parts of the fillet, and very little on the thinner tail end.

Lay a sheet of plastic wrap (large enough to enclose the halibut in a double thickness) on the work surface. Turn the fillet over onto the plastic wrap, and wrap it up. Place the fish on a tray in the fridge, with a wooden board or baking tray on top to exert a light pressure.

To serve, remove the plastic wrap. Rinse the halibut under cold running water and use your fingertips to check that all the salt and sugar mixture and most of the dill is washed off. Dry the halibut thoroughly on a dish towel, sprinkle the flesh side with the dill reserved for the garnish, and press with your fingertips to make it adhere.

Using a very sharp, fine-bladed knife, slice the halibut very thinly, as you would smoked salmon, and serve on individual plates, with lemon wedges.

marinated mackerel diamonds

These can be served as a warm hors d'oeuvre; leave them in the marinade for only 30 minutes, then steam them for 3 to 5 minutes, depending on their thickness. Boiled baby new potatoes make a good accompaniment.

Serves 6

6 mackerel fillets

1/2 lemon

10 juniper berries, lightly crushed

leaves from 1 thyme sprig

1 quantity sweet–sour marinade (page 14)

salt and freshly ground pepper

Pull out any pin bones from the mackerel with tweezers, then cut the fillets into large diamonds and put them in a deep dish. Season lightly.

Cut the lemon half vertically through the middle, then slice it into thin semicircles. Place these in between the mackerel diamonds, then scatter over the crushed juniper and thyme.

Pour the marinade over the mackerel diamonds. Cover with plastic wrap and leave at room temperature until completely cold, then refrigerate for 2 to 3 hours.

Serve the mackerel straight from the dish, allowing everyone to season their own fish. Freshly toasted rustic bread is the perfect accompaniment.

PREPARING SCALLOPS

Hold the shell flat-side down with the fingertips of one hand. Using your other hand, slide a rigid knife blade between the two shells.

Carefully run the blade along the inner surface of the flat shell to detach and separate the scallop from the shell.

Lift off the top shell. Slide a spoon or a small metal spatula under the scallop in the concave shell, and remove it.

Using your thumb and index finger, carefully pull away the frilly membrane, and remove the small muscle attached to the scallop. Detach the coral.

The scallop is now ready to use. Rinse it under cold running water. The coral can be used separately or with the scallop, depending on your chosen recipe.

scallops marinated in lemon-scented olive oil

Crisp textured, finely sliced, raw zucchini contrasts beautifully with the melting softness of sliced scallops. For a special occasion, try replacing the salt flakes with grains of caviar ... and enjoy the accolade from your guests.

Serves 4

8 very fresh white sea scallops, total weight about 1 pound
1/2 cup olive oil
juice of 3 lemons
1/3 cup snipped basil
3 small, long, firm zucchini
3 oranges, preferably blood oranges
sea salt flakes
salt and freshly ground pepper

Cut the scallops into slices, 1/8 inch thick. Spread them in a single layer on a tray and season very lightly with salt, and generously with pepper. Mix 5 tablespoons of the olive oil with the lemon juice, and sprinkle evenly over the scallop slices. Cover with plastic wrap, and refrigerate for 10 minutes.

Turn the scallop slices, one at a time, in the marinade, then scatter over the basil. Cover again with plastic wrap and refrigerate for 5 minutes.

Meanwhile, score along the length of the zucchini with a zesting knife, several times to make evenly spaced grooves, then cut into slices, 1/16 to 1/8 inch thick. Peel and segment the oranges, discarding all pith.

To serve, arrange 6 orange segments in a rosette in the center of each plate, and place the zucchini disks around them. Sprinkle with a little olive oil and scatter on a few salt flakes, then place a scallop slice on each zucchini disk. Serve immediately.

Salmon tartare:

1/2 pound skinless middle-cut salmon fillet
1 to 2 cornichons or small gherkins, very finely diced
3 tablespoons finely snipped dill, plus extra to garnish
4 tender green parts of scallions, finely snipped
3 tablespoons chive oil (page 188)
lemon juice, to taste

To serve:

1/2 cucumber
4 red endive or radicchio leaves
4 white Belgian endive leaves
4 lemon verbena sprigs (optional)
1/2 quantity green olive and lemon salsa (page 24), optional

tartares of salmon and scallops in endive leaves

I love this unusual presentation. Serving the two tartares in different colored Belgian endive leaves makes an attractive contrast, though you can, of course, use all one color. As with all raw dishes, the ingredients for these tartares must be perfectly fresh. Serve within half an hour of preparation, to preserve the fresh flavors. You can adjust the quantity of lemon juice to suit your taste. I like to drizzle a little green olive and lemon salsa (page 24) over the two tartares for a touch of piquancy.

Serves 4

Scallop tartare:

4 sea scallops, in the shell if possible
1 teaspoon dried pink peppercorns
3 tablespoons finely snipped chives
2 1/2 tablespoons small capers
2 tablespoons orange oil (page 188)
lemon juice, to taste
salt and freshly ground pepper

To make the scallop tartare, open the scallops and remove the white meat (see page 39); you should have about ½ pound. Cut the scallops into very thin slices, about ⅛ inch thick. Cut these slices into ⅛-inch strips, then into ⅛-inch dice. Place in a bowl.

Lightly crush the pink peppercorns between your fingertips and sprinkle over the scallops. Add the chives, capers, orange oil, and lemon juice to taste. Season lightly with salt and pepper. Stir carefully to mix, cover with plastic wrap, and keep in the fridge until ready to serve.

For the salmon tartare, cut the salmon into ⅛-inch dice (in the same way as the scallops). Place in a bowl, add the diced cornichons, snipped dill, scallion leaves, chive oil, and lemon juice to taste. Season lightly with salt and pepper. Mix with a spoon, cover with plastic wrap, and refrigerate until needed.

Peel, halve, and seed the cucumber. Cut the cucumber flesh into long thin "spaghetti" shreds. Make a little pile of cucumber spaghetti on each serving plate.

Trim the endive leaves to form canoe shapes. Fill the red leaves with scallop tartare, and the white leaves with salmon tartare. Place one of each color on each serving plate and scatter a little dill over the salmon tartare. Garnish the plate with lemon verbena, if available. Spoon the salsa (if serving) into tiny dishes and place on the plates.

escabèche

Escabèche originated in the Mediterranean and is traditionally prepared with fish from that region, such as sardines and anchovies. When game is in season, I make an innovative version, using partridge breasts or tiny plump quail, adjusting the marinating and cooking times accordingly.

Serves 6

6 very fresh small sardines
6 very fresh anchovies
4 tablespoons olive oil
salt and freshly ground pepper

Marinade:

1 lemon
3 carrots, peeled
2 shallots, peeled
3 tablespoons olive oil
1 tablespoon white peppercorns, crushed
leaves from a large thyme sprig
2 bay leaves
2 garlic cloves, peeled and crushed
1 tablespoon coriander seeds, crushed
pinch of cayenne pepper
6 tablespoons top-quality white or red wine vinegar
1 2/3 cups water

Gently scrape off the scales from the sardines with your thumbnail. Cut off the heads with a knife and slit open the belly, leaving the tail intact. Push out the guts with your thumb and lift out the backbone with your fingers, or a knife. Prepare the anchovies in the same way; there is no need to scale them.

Wipe the sardines and anchovies with a damp cloth, lay them skin-side down on the work surface, and open out like a book or butterfly. Season with salt and pepper.

Heat the olive oil in a deep frying pan set over a high heat. Put in the butterflied sardines, skin-side down, and quickly color them over a high heat for 30 seconds. Lift them out with a slotted spatula onto the serving platter and leave at room temperature.

Repeat with the anchovies, coloring them for 15 seconds. Discard the oil left in the pan.

For the marinade, cut the lemon into 1/16-inch slices, discarding the ends. Cut grooves along the length of the carrots using a zesting knife, then cut into thin rounds. Finely slice the shallots.

Heat the olive oil in the frying pan. Add the shallots and carrots and sweat over a medium heat for a minute or two. Add all the other marinade ingredients, bring to a boil and bubble for 1 minute. Skim the surface if necessary, season very lightly with salt, then pour the boiling marinade over the sardines and anchovies. Leave until cold, then refrigerate for 2 to 3 hours.

Bring the escabèche to room temperature half an hour before serving. Bring the dish to the table and let everyone help themselves. Serve with slices of crusty country bread.

carpaccio of cèpes

Cèpes in prime condition are essential for this simple dish, which makes a delicious, light hors d'oeuvre.

Serves 6

12 very fresh, firm-textured cèpes or porcini mushrooms (boletus), preferably small
juice of 2 lemons
1/2 cup plus 2 tablespoons olive oil
5 tablespoons finely chopped shallots
2 lemon thyme sprigs, leaves stripped
5 ounces tomatoes, peeled, seeded, and finely diced
3 1/2 ounces very dry chorizo sausage, skinned
2 tablespoons snipped flat-leaf parsley
salt and freshly ground pepper

Using a small knife, trim the cèpe stalks, and cut off any traces of earth, or impurities. Wipe the cèpes gently with a slightly damp cloth, and refrigerate.

In a bowl, mix the lemon juice, olive oil, shallot, thyme leaves, and diced tomatoes with a little salt.

When ready to serve, cut the cèpes into 3/16-inch slices. Arrange them attractively on serving plates and drizzle with the dressing. Using a Parmesan grater, grate the chorizo over the top. Sprinkle with the parsley and a grinding of pepper. Serve chilled.

lightly smoked duck breasts with bok choy

My travels to the Far East have influenced my cooking in recent years. Smoking duck breasts accentuates their fine flavor and the oriental aromatics add a special something. This utterly sublime dish is excellent for lunch or dinner.

You will need a heavy casserole, about 12 inches in diameter and at least 6 inches deep, with a tight-fitting lid; a 4- to 8-inch quiche ring and a 10-inch round wire rack. It is essential to protect the base and lid of the casserole with foil, as the sugary smoke could damage them.

Serves 4

*4 boneless duckling breasts (preferably Long Island
or Challandais)
coarse sea salt
coarsely crushed peppercorns
6 star anise
2 dried orange zests (see page 113)
2 cups Demerara or light brown sugar
1¹/4 pounds bok choy or Chinese cabbage
1 red bell pepper
6 tablespoons sugar syrup (page 188)
3 tablespoons untoasted sesame oil
salt and freshly ground pepper*

Half an hour before smoking the duck breasts, make criss-cross incisions all over the skin with the tip of a knife. Sprinkle with salt and crushed peppercorns and set aside. Grind the star anise, dried orange zest, and Demerara sugar together in a spice grinder or food processor to a fine powder.

To prepare the smoker, line the base and underside of the casserole lid with foil. Put in the quiche ring, then sprinkle the ground spice mixture over the foil. Place the wire rack on the ring.

Wipe off the excess salt and pepper from the duck breasts and arrange them skin-side up on the rack. Put on the lid and place the casserole over a high heat. As soon as a light smoke seeps out, lower the heat and cook for 8 to 10 minutes.

Take off the heat and move the lid slightly so as to barely uncover the casserole. Leave for 10 minutes, then transfer the duck breasts to a plate.

Blanch the bok choy in boiling water for 30 seconds to 1 minute, depending on size. Drain thoroughly. Halve, core, and seed the red pepper, then cut into julienne. Heat the sugar syrup in a pan, add the red pepper and simmer for 3 minutes to candy; drain.

Heat the sesame oil in a wok and stir-fry the bok choy for 3 or 4 minutes, keeping it crunchy. Add the red pepper julienne and turn off the heat.

To serve, cut the duck lengthwise into thin slices, using a sharp knife. Arrange the bok choy on one side of each serving plate and fan out the sliced duck breasts alongside. Serve immediately.

smoked chicken wings

Chicken wings can be smoked in the same way as duck breasts (above), allowing an extra 4 minutes smoking. Just before serving, I brush the wings with runny honey, lightly flavored with lemon juice and a pinch of cayenne pepper, and glaze them under a hot broiler for 5 minutes. Finally, I sprinkle them with toasted sesame seeds. They are delicious served on their own as nibbles, or with salad leaves as a starter.

lightly smoked mussels

These delicately smoked mussels are divine tossed with pasta and served drizzled with pesto (see page 88), as illustrated. They can also be added at the last moment to a seafood risotto (page 94). For a light, refreshing starter, toss them in a lemon and mint vinaigrette (page 17) and serve with tomato wedges and frisée (curly endive).

The mussels can be smoked several hours in advance. Cover them with plastic wrap so that they don't dry out, keep in the fridge and steam for a few minutes just before serving.

Serves 4 as a starter
2¹/4 pounds live mussels (preferably blue mussels, Bouchot, or Shetland)
3 star anise
dried lemon zest from 1 lemon (see page 113)
1¹/4 cups Demerara or light brown sugar

Scrub the mussels, wash in several changes of water and drain. Grind the star anise, dried lemon zest, and Demerara sugar together in a spice grinder or food processor to a fine powder.

Prepare the smoker as for lightly smoked duck breasts (page 44). Put in the mussels and smoke for 6 to 8 minutes, until they have all opened, then turn off the heat and move the lid very slightly so as to barely uncover the casserole. After about 10 minutes, shell almost all of the mussels, keeping a few in the half-shell for garnish. Discard any unopened mussels.

lightly smoked scallops

Follow the method for lightly smoked mussels (above), allowing 4 to 6 minutes smoking, depending on the size of the scallops. The smoked scallops can be steamed for 3 to 4 minutes, or pan-fried in clarified butter (page 188) for 2 to 3 minutes, again depending on size. To serve, spread a spoonful of my herb salsa (page 24) on a plate, top with the scallops, and surround with corn salad or arugula leaves.

smoked sea bass with chive nage

Light smoking brings out the flavor of this fish, and subtly permeates it with the aroma of the wood. You will need a smoker, about 2¼ pounds charcoal briquettes, and 2 handfuls of oak, beech, or chestnut sawdust.

Serves 4
1 very fresh unskinned fillet of sea bass, about 1¹/4 pounds
14 ounces fine sugar snap peas, topped and tailed
¹/2 cup snipped chives
5 tablespoons butter, finely diced
5 lemon wedges
salt and freshly ground pepper

Check that there are no bones left in the fish; rinse and pat dry. Make 6 evenly spaced small diagonal incisions across the middle two-thirds of the fillet on the skin side.

Put the briquettes in a metal shovel under a direct heat source, or into a lit barbecue. When glowing, put in the smoker box and sprinkle with sawdust. Lay the fish, skin-side down, on the grill of the smoker, close the box lid and leave for 10 to 20 minutes, according to the degree of smoking desired. Lift the fish onto a wire rack and let stand for 15 minutes. If not using at once, wrap and refrigerate for up to 24 hours.

To cook the fish, cut it into 4 portions. Half-fill a steamer pan with water and salt lightly. Bring to a boil, lower the heat to a simmer, and position the top part of the steamer. Put in the sea bass pieces, skin-side down, season, cover, and steam for 3 to 4 minutes. Add the sugar snap peas and cook for another 2 to 3 minutes. To check if the fish is cooked, insert a fine knife tip into the thickest part for 10 seconds; it should penetrate easily, and feel hot when you take it out.

For the sauce, put 5 tablespoons of the cooking water in a small pan and reduce by one-third. Add the chives and whisk in the butter, a piece at a time. Squeeze in the juice from 1 lemon wedge; season to taste.

Serve the fish with the chive sauce poured over, and accompanied by the sugar snaps and lemon wedges.

eggs, crêpes, and soufflés

At the age of barely three, each time I heard our solitary hen Julie cackle that she was about to lay, I would rush to collect the still-warm egg and take it to my mother, cradling it gently in both hands. I was always surprised and fascinated by the warmth of a new-laid egg. I had no idea then that the egg and I would develop such a long and fruitful partnership throughout my life. An egg is a rich, concentrated source of nutrients – a meal in itself – and I love and respect it in all its forms. In fact I eat about twenty eggs a week in one guise or another.

tortillas, frittatas, and eggah. According to what is fresh in the market, I make them with asparagus tips, anchovy fillets, or confit eggplant, to serve in wedges with a little tomato coulis; simplicity itself on a plate.

When making soufflés, it is important to use the correct amount of egg white; too little and it won't rise properly, resulting in a heavy texture; too much, and it will taste horribly bland. To achieve the desired flavor and lightness, I find it more precise to measure or weigh the egg whites rather than count them, because eggs vary in weight so much. I base my soufflés on an average 2-ounce egg (comprising just under ¾ ounce of yolk, 1¼ ounces of white and about ⅙ ounce of shell). If a soufflé calls for 4 egg whites, for example, you need 5 ounces (⅔ cup) in total. My advice is to keep a cool

It is always important to use very fresh eggs. To check the freshness, I pour a quart of water into a bowl, add ½ cup salt and put in two or three eggs. If they roll around on the bottom, they are ultra-fresh; if they float slightly, they are a few days old, but still useable, but if they float on the surface, I throw them away.

Sugar and salt are the enemies of raw egg yolks and will burn them on contact unless you beat them immediately with a whisk or fork. As for the whites, the white of a new-laid egg will not rise properly when beaten, but one that has been refrigerated for several days will puff up into a perfect snow. Frozen whites can be beaten even stiffer, so I recommend that you freeze any leftover egg whites to use for meringues, macaroons, mousses, and of course, soufflés.

In Algeria, I learned to master delicious flat omelets called eggah. Now I compose all sorts of seasonal variations – a veritable waltz of

head and treat a soufflé like any other dish. They are easy and docile; just follow the techniques that I use. My visitor's book is full of eulogies extolling my soufflés ... one lady guest remarked that her soufflé was better than an orgasm!

Making crêpes couldn't be easier. All you need is a frying pan, preferably nonstick. Cook the crêpes, pile them on a plate and let them perfume your kitchen. Fill savory herb crêpes (page 58) with little treasures, like seafood, tomatoes, or confit peppers and serve them warm – delicious! Or cover sweet crêpes with grated chocolate or jam, roll up and watch children devour them. To make edible baskets for serving ice cream and sorbet, brush one side of a thin sweet crêpe with melted *couverture* chocolate, drape it in a bowl, coated-side inwards, and leave until hardened. Fill with ice cream, sorbet, or orange segments topped with candied peel.

creamy scrambled eggs with baby vegetables à la grecque

This combination may seem surprising, but it makes an attractive spring or summer dish, and the flavor is sublime. It should be served cold, not chilled. Any spare dressing can be kept in a sealed jar in the fridge for at least a week.

Serves 4

À la grecque dressing:

3 tablespoons white wine vinegar
1/2 cup olive oil
1/2 cup water
1/2 teaspoon coriander seeds, crushed
1/2 teaspoon white peppercorns, crushed
3 tablespoons concentrated tomato paste
5 tablespoons lemon juice
2 garlic cloves, peeled and crushed
1 small bouquet garni
1/4 cup sugar

Vegetables:

4 baby fennel bulbs, trimmed
4 baby zucchini, halved lengthwise
24 slim green beans
8 radishes
8 small scallions
8 small button mushrooms

Scrambled eggs:

4 tablespoons butter
8 eggs
1/4 cup heavy cream
salt and freshly ground pepper

To garnish:

4 bundles of 10 to 12 chives
2 tablespoons snipped chives

Put all the ingredients for the à la grecque dressing in a saucepan over a low heat, add salt, and simmer gently for 20 minutes, stirring occasionally with a whisk.

Blanch all the vegetables except the mushrooms separately in boiling water. Allow 2 minutes for the fennel, and about 30 seconds for the zucchini, green beans, radishes, and scallions. Drain and add salt to taste.

Add all the vegetables to the dressing and simmer for 5 minutes. Discard the bouquet garni, tip the vegetables into a bowl, and leave to cool at room temperature.

To prepare the scrambled eggs, melt the butter in a saucepan over a gentle heat. Break the eggs into a bowl, season with salt and pepper and beat lightly with a fork. Pour into the saucepan and cook over a very low heat, stirring gently and continuously with a wooden spoon until the eggs are scrambled and just cooked to your taste. Transfer them to a bowl, cover with plastic wrap, and cool at room temperature.

When the eggs are cold, whip the cream to a ribbon consistency and delicately fold into the eggs. Spoon them onto 4 serving plates. Using a slotted spoon, lift the vegetables from the dressing and arrange them around the eggs. Drizzle with a few drops of dressing. Garnish each plate with a bundle of chives, and scatter the snipped chives over the scrambled eggs to serve.

scrambled eggs with crab

Cook the eggs as above until just scrambled to your liking. Take off the heat, add the whipped cream, then scatter 5 ounces fresh white crabmeat over the mixture. Mix gently and season to taste with salt and pepper. Divide between 4 warmed plates, and scatter 6 to 8 capers and a pinch of snipped chives over each serving. Serve at once.

POACHING EGGS

It is essential to use only very fresh eggs so that the whites completely cover the yolks. You can generally poach 4 eggs at a time. Three-quarters fill a shallow pan, about 2 inches deep, with water and bring to a boil. Add 2 tablespoons white wine vinegar. Don't add salt to the water, or the egg whites will become pitted with tiny holes. Break an egg into a teacup and tip it very gently into the water at the point where it is bubbling. Add the other 3 eggs, one at a time, in this way and poach for about 2 minutes, according to how soft you like your eggs.

Use a small slotted spoon to lift out the first egg and press with your fingertip to check if it is properly cooked. If so, slip it into a bowl of ice water to prevent further cooking. Do the same with the other eggs.

Trim the eggs into a neat cushion shape. Hold the egg in your hand and pare off the untidy edges with a sharp knife (see below).

If you want to serve the eggs immediately, drain them on a dish towel.

If you want to serve them later, leave them in the ice water in the fridge. To reheat the eggs, put them in an empty bowl, carefully cover with boiling water and leave for 15 to 20 seconds (not a moment longer, or they will go hard). This way, you can even poach your eggs the day before for breakfast the next morning.

poached eggs on watercress salad with red pepper salsa

This is the simplest dish imaginable, but its refreshing taste and vibrant colors make it highly original.

Serves 4

4 slices of baguette, cut on the diagonal
1/2 pound tender watercress sprigs
4 tablespoons lemon and mint vinaigrette (page 17)
8 poached eggs (see left)
1/2 quantity red pepper salsa (page 22)
12 basil leaves
seeds from 1/2 pomegranate
salt and freshly ground pepper

Toast the baguette slices just before assembling the dish. Dress the watercress with the vinaigrette and arrange it in the middle of 4 serving plates. Lay a toasted baguette slice diagonally across the watercress. Season the eggs with salt and pepper, place on the toast, and spoon on a little red pepper salsa.

Arrange 3 basil leaves on one side of each plate and spoon the rest of the salsa around them. Scatter a few pomegranate seeds over the watercress.

poached eggs with fondant white onions

Thinly slice 24 small white salad onions, and sweat in 6 tablespoons butter over a low heat, until meltingly tender. Lightly brown 4 thin slices of baguette in clarified butter (page 188), spread with a little of the fondant onions, top with a poached egg, and cover thickly with the remaining onions. Sprinkle with snipped flat-leaf parsley and serve immediately.

tomato omelet

This is a tomato omelet as you have never seen one before. Slitting it open to reveal the vivid red filling makes for mouth-watering anticipation. It is also delicious served cold for an unusual summer lunch or picnic dish.

Serves 2

Filling:

1/2 pound tomatoes
1 tablespoon olive oil
1 garlic clove, peeled (optional)
a few basil leaves (optional)

Omelet:

5 eggs
2 tablespoons clarified butter (page 188)
salt and freshly ground pepper
thyme sprig, to garnish

To make the filling, peel, halve, seed, and dice the tomatoes. Heat the olive oil in a pan, add the tomatoes and cook gently for about 3 minutes, depending on how ripe they are. If using, add the garlic at this stage and remove it when the tomatoes are cooked. Season lightly and keep on one side. Add the basil, if you like.

To make the omelet, break the eggs into a bowl and season with salt and pepper. Add a spoonful of clarified butter and beat lightly with a fork.

Heat a frying pan (preferably nonstick), about 8 inches in diameter, until very hot. Add the remaining butter and spread it over the surface of the pan. Quickly pour the eggs into the pan. Using the side of the fork so as not to scratch the surface of the pan, keep stirring the eggs with one hand while shaking the pan with the other. When the omelet is set underneath, but still runny on top, spoon the tomato filling in a line along the middle.

Tilt and shake the pan away from you to push one half of the omelet towards the middle. Roll the omelet onto a serving plate.

With the tip of a knife, cut it lengthwise down the middle to reveal the tomatoes (and add any leftover filling). Garnish with a sprig of thyme and brush the omelet with a touch of clarified butter to give it a sheen. Serve immediately.

variations

There is almost no limit to what you can put in an omelet, so be creative! Delicious fillings to add at the last moment, just before rolling the omelet, include:
• mussels *à la marinière*, either plain or tossed in a little garlicky butter
• strips of smoked salmon which permeate the eggs to give a superb flavor
• ratatouille made with tiny diced vegetables
• diced bacon fried with baby onions, for a substantial *omelette grand'mère*

eggah with grilled merguez

My interpretation of this rustic Moroccan dish reminds me of the time I spent in North Africa, and I often make it when I am at my house in the South of France.

Cook the eggah in a heatproof cast-iron, earthenware or porcelain dish, about 8 inches in diameter and 1¾ inches deep, and serve it straight from the dish. It is also good served cold for brunch; keep it in the larder or a cool place overnight, not in the fridge as this would deaden the flavors.

Serves 4

4 small merguez sausages, or other spicy sausages
1 medium-large tomato (4 ounces)
1 large or 2 small potatoes (6 ounces)
4 tablespoons olive oil
2 garlic cloves, peeled and crushed
¹/₂ teaspoon harissa paste
8 eggs
1 teaspoon ground cumin
about 10 cardamom seeds
2 tablespoons snipped flat-leaf parsley
salt and freshly ground pepper

Preheat the oven to 350°F. Heat a griddle pan until very hot, add the merguez sausages and turn to brown on all sides; they should be two-thirds cooked. Cut them in half, place on a plate, and keep at room temperature.

Peel, seed, and dice the tomato. Peel and dice the potatoes. Heat 2 tablespoons olive oil in a nonstick frying pan and sauté the potatoes over a medium heat until golden and cooked. Add the garlic, cook for another 2 to 3 minutes, then put in the tomato and harissa. Cook gently for another 5 minutes.

Put the remaining oil in the heatproof dish and place on a heat diffuser over a medium heat.

Lightly beat the eggs with the cumin, cardamom seeds, and a little salt and pepper.

When the oil is hot, add the egg mixture and cook, stirring with a fork, as if you were making an omelet, but over a lower heat. When the eggs are half-set, add the potato and tomato mixture and mix them delicately into the eggs, then push the merguez sausages halfway into the eggah.

Cook in the oven for 6 to 8 minutes, depending how well you like your eggs cooked. Sprinkle with parsley and serve straight from the dish.

eggah with fava beans and tagliatelle

Serves 4

1/2 pound tagliatelle (preferably fresh, see page 84)
8 eggs
4 tablespoons olive oil
1 garlic clove, peeled and finely chopped
14 ounces fava beans (weight in the pod),
shelled, skinned, and blanched
salt and freshly ground pepper

Preheat the oven to 350°F. Cook the tagliatelle in boiling water until *al dente*; drain thoroughly and cut into 4-inch lengths. Lightly beat the eggs with a little salt and pepper.

Heat the olive oil in a heatproof dish (preferably cast-iron), add the tagliatelle, and fry until lightly browned. Add the garlic, pour on the eggs, and cook as for eggah with grilled merguez (see left). Sprinkle on the fava beans, and cook in the oven for 4 to 6 minutes, until done to your liking. Serve very hot, straight from the dish.

parmesan and sorrel frittata

The freshness and acidity of sorrel counterbalances rich Parmesan, and transforms this simple Italian frittata into a luscious lunch. Alternatively, you can cut it into diamonds and serve it as tapas.

Serves 4

5 tablespoons butter
1/2 pound sorrel, stalks removed, and washed
12 eggs
2 tablespoons olive oil
31/2 ounces Parmesan cheese, freshly grated
1 tablespoon clarified butter (page 188)
salt and freshly ground pepper

Melt 2 tablespoons of the butter in a small saucepan, add the sorrel, and wilt over a high heat for 1 minute. Immediately take off the heat, drain the sorrel and tip it into a bowl.

Beat the eggs in a bowl and season very lightly with salt and pepper. Heat the rest of the butter and the olive oil in a frying pan (preferably nonstick). When very hot, add the eggs, and cook as you would an omelet, stirring delicately every minute with the side of a fork until half-cooked.

Spread the sorrel over the surface, and sprinkle with Parmesan, still stirring delicately with the fork. Lower the heat and cook until the frittata is set and pale golden underneath, then invert it onto a lightly buttered plate. Slide it back into the pan and cook on the other side for 2 to 3 minutes, until pale golden and done to your liking.

Slide the frittata onto a serving plate and brush the surface with a little clarified butter. Serve at once.

snail and herb frittata

Omit the sorrel and cheese. Pan-fry some snails in butter lightly flavored with garlic. Meanwhile, half-cook the eggs as above. Scatter the pan-fried snails over the half-cooked eggs with a handful of snipped fresh herbs, and finish as above.

herb crêpes

These crêpes are so versatile. I use them in dishes, such as my wild mushroom and baby vegetable terrines (pages 76–7), and châteaubriand in a brioche crust (page 138). You can also fill them with savory mixtures for an easy lunch or supper.

For an unusual dish, cook some merguez sausages on the grill, or fry over a high heat in a nonstick frying pan. At the last moment, brush herb crêpes with a little Dijon mustard, drizzle with maple syrup, and roll them round the sausages. This elegant way of serving merguez really brings out their flavor.

Makes six 11- or 12-inch crêpes
1/2 cup flour
2/3 cup milk
2 eggs
1 tablespoon chopped or snipped herbs
salt and freshly ground pepper

For cooking:
1/2 small new potato
2 tablespoons clarified butter (page 188)

Put the flour in a bowl and make a well in the middle. Add one-third of the milk, the eggs, a pinch of salt, and a grinding of pepper. Mix lightly with a whisk to make a smooth batter, then stir in the rest of the milk. Cover with plastic wrap and leave to rest for at least 30 minutes. Stir the herbs into the batter just before cooking.

To cook the crêpes, heat an 11- or 12-inch crêpe pan or skillet. Spear the rounded side of the potato with a fork, dip into the clarified butter and slide the flat side over the hot pan surface to grease it; remove.

Stir the batter, then ladle just enough into the pan to cover the base. Cook quickly for about 1 minute, then toss the crêpe or turn it over with a palette knife and cook the other side for barely a minute. Make another 5 crêpes in the same way.

Stack the cooked crêpes on a plate, interleaving with wax or parchment paper between each one to prevent them from sticking together.

seafood crêpes

Vary the seafood according to taste and availability, using scallops or shrimp instead of langoustines, or clams instead of mussels, for example. Laver has a surprisingly delicious iodine flavor. I think of it as the spice from the sea. (Recipe illustrated on page 19.)

Serves 6
six 7-inch herb crêpes (see left)
24 medium or large langoustines (or jumbo shrimp)
6 tablespoons dry white wine
48 live mussels, cleaned
48 small button mushroom caps, wiped clean
2 tablespoons butter
juice of 1 lemon
2 cups sauce suprême, made with fish stock (page 18)
2 pieces laver seaweed, rinsed (optional)
salt and freshly ground pepper
lemon wedges, to serve

Plunge the *langoustines* into a large pan of boiling salted water. As soon as it returns to a boil, turn off the heat, leave for 3 minutes, then drain. Cool, shell them, and place in a bowl; cover with a damp cloth.

Put the wine in the pan and set over a high heat. Add the mussels, cover tightly, and cook for 2 to 3 minutes, shaking the pan. As soon as they open, remove and drain, reserving the juice. Shell the mussels, place in a bowl, and keep covered. Decant the liquid into a small pan, leaving behind any grit. Reduce over a medium heat to about 3 tablespoons; strain and reserve.

Put the mushrooms, butter, and half the lemon juice in a pan. Barely cover with cold water, salt lightly, and bring to a boil. Immediately turn off the heat; set aside.

Gently reheat the sauce suprême, stirring. Add the mussel liquid and cook gently for 5 minutes. Add the remaining lemon juice and check the seasoning.

Blanch the seaweed, if using, in boiling water for 1 minute. Drain and tear each piece into six. Add half to the sauce, along with the mussels, *langoustines,* and mushrooms. Heat gently for 5 minutes without boiling, stirring delicately from time to time.

Fill the warm crêpes with the seafood and sauce. Serve with the remaining seaweed and lemon wedges.

millefeuille of crêpes soufflées with red currants

This is yummy. It is best served as soon as it's assembled – you will need a long knife with a fine, sharp blade to cut it. It will be easier to cut if you place it in the freezer for 30 minutes or so before cutting, to firm up the filling. For an extra treat, serve the millefeuille with red currant and passion fruit coulis (page 28).

Serves 6 to 8

Crêpes soufflées:

1/2 cup plus 1 tablespoon flour
1/2 cup milk
2 egg yolks
pinch of salt
2 tablespoons sugar, plus a pinch
3 egg whites
3 tablespoons clarified butter (page 188)

Filling:

1/2 cup heavy cream
1 cup crème pâtissière (page 181)
1 pound red currants, stalks removed

To decorate:

confectioners' sugar, to dust
few clusters of red currants

To assemble the millefeuille, you need a 6-inch quiche ring that is 2 inches deep. Line it with a triple thick band of parchment paper that is about 5 inches deep (to extend above the ring) and secure with tape.

To make the crêpe soufflée batter, put the flour into a bowl and make a well in the middle. Add two-thirds of the milk, the egg yolks, and a pinch each of salt and sugar. Mix gently with a balloon whisk until smooth, then stir in the remaining milk.

Beat the egg whites in a clean bowl until soft peaks form, then add the 2 tablespoons sugar and beat until stiff. Gently fold into the crêpe soufflée batter.

Heat 2 teaspoons clarified butter in a 6- or 8-inch frying pan until very hot. Pour in one-fifth of the batter and tilt the pan to make a crêpe soufflé about ⅝ inch thick. Cook for about 1½ to 2 minutes, until golden underneath, then carefully turn it over with a palette knife and cook the other side for about 1½ minutes. Place the crêpe soufflée on a sheet of wax paper and cook another four in the same way. If necessary, trim the crêpes so that they will fit inside the prepared quiche ring, using a sharp knife.

For the filling, whip the cream to soft peaks, then fold into the crème pâtissière. Spoon into a pastry bag fitted with a ¾-inch plain tip.

Put the prepared quiche ring on a serving plate and lay a crêpe inside, to make the base. Starting at the center and working towards the edge, pipe a spiral of cream filling, about ⅝ inch thick. Scatter over about a quarter of the red currants. Pipe a layer of cream on top as before, then cover with a second crêpe. Repeat the process three times, finishing with the fifth and final crêpe.

Refrigerate the millefeuille for up to 3 hours before serving, or pop it into the freezer for 30 minutes.

To serve, carefully remove the quiche ring and lining paper in one deft movement. If necessary, smooth the edges with a palette knife. Dust with confectioners' sugar and top with clusters of red currants. Serve right away.

chocolate crêpes

These crêpes are delectable served warm, with a coffee sabayon (page 31), whipped cream, or vanilla ice cream. They also feature in my peppermint soufflé in a chocolate crêpe (page 64).

Makes twelve 6-inch crêpes
1 cup flour
¼ cup unsweetened cocoa powder
1⅔ cups milk
2 eggs
¼ cup sugar
pinch of salt
½ cup heavy cream

For cooking:
½ small new potato
2 tablespoons clarified butter (page 188)

Sift the flour and cocoa powder together into a bowl and make a well. Pour in one-third of the milk, break in the eggs, and add the sugar and salt. Mix gently with a whisk to make a smooth batter, then stir in the cream and the rest of the milk. Strain through a sieve into a bowl. Cover with plastic wrap and let rest for at least 30 minutes.

To cook the crêpes, heat a 6- or 7-inch crêpe pan or skillet. Spear the rounded side of the potato with a fork, dip into the clarified butter and slide over the surface of the hot pan to grease it; remove.

Stir the batter, then ladle just enough into the pan to cover the base. Cook quickly for about 1 minute, then toss the crêpe or turn it over with a palette knife and cook on the other side for barely a minute. Cook all the crêpes in the same way and stack them on a plate, interleaving with wax or parchment paper to prevent them from sticking together. Serve warm.

smoked haddock soufflé with poached egg "en surprise"

This soufflé has featured on the winter menu at The Waterside Inn for many years. Our regular customers never tire of it; the mingling of the runny yolk – from the hidden poached egg – with the smoked haddock is a source of delight.

Serves 4

Béchamel:
2 tablespoons butter, softened
4 tablespoons flour
1²/3 cups milk

Soufflé:
6 egg yolks
3 tablespoons butter, softened
5 ounces Gruyère, finely grated
4¹/2 ounces smoked haddock fillet
1²/3 cups heavy cream
8 egg whites (about 1¹/4 cups)
1 tablespoon snipped dill
4 poached eggs (page 54)
salt and freshly ground pepper

Garnish:
4 poached quail's eggs
4 dill sprigs

Preheat the oven to 425°F. To make the béchamel, melt the butter in a small heavy-based saucepan. Off the heat, stir in the flour, then return the pan to a low heat and cook for 3 minutes, stirring continuously with a small whisk. Off the heat, pour in the milk, stirring. Place on a medium heat and bring to a boil, stirring all the time. Lower the heat and simmer for about 10 minutes, still stirring continuously.

Off the heat, mix the 6 egg yolks into the béchamel, and season with salt and pepper. Cover this soufflé base with plastic wrap and set aside at room temperature.

Grease the insides of 4 individual 4-inch soufflé dishes, 2½ inches deep, with softened butter. Sprinkle a small handful of grated Gruyère into one soufflé dish, rotate it to coat the inside, then tip the excess into a second dish. Repeat the process to coat all 4 dishes.

Put the smoked haddock into a small saucepan, pour on the cream, and place over a low heat. When the cream starts bubbling, lower the heat to a gentle simmer and cook for 5 minutes. Turn off the heat and leave until cool enough to handle, then remove the skin and flake the fish with your fingertips, removing any small bones. Leave the fish in the cream.

In a clean bowl, beat the egg whites with a pinch of salt to soft peaks. Whisk one-third of the egg whites into the soufflé base to loosen it.

Add this mixture to the remaining egg whites and fold in delicately, using a spatula, adding the Gruyère and dill as you go.

At this point, cover the poached eggs with boiling water for 15 seconds to warm them, then drain on paper towels.

Half-fill each prepared dish with the soufflé mixture, then spoon in the creamy haddock mix.

Put a poached egg in the middle and fill the dishes with the remaining soufflé mixture to come slightly above the top. Smooth the surface with a palette knife.

Run a knife around the edge of the mixture to ease it away from the side of the dish; this helps the soufflé to rise. Stand the soufflé dishes in a roasting pan and pour in enough boiling water to come halfway up the sides. Cook in the oven for 6 minutes.

Top each soufflé with a quail's egg and a sprig of dill, and serve immediately.

grand marnier and mango soufflés

Sometimes I top these individual sweet soufflés with a few very thin strands of orange zest lightly poached in sugar syrup, or a spoonful of passion fruit seeds. The sharp piquancy adds an elusive quality to their delicacy and lightness.

Serves 4

2 tablespoons butter, softened
³⁄4 cup plus 2 tablespoons sugar
1 cup milk
1 vanilla bean, split lengthwise
3 egg yolks
3 tablespoons potato flour
7 tablespoons Grand Marnier
³⁄4 cup diced very ripe mango flesh
7 egg whites (about 1¹⁄8 cups)
confectioners' sugar, to dust

Brush the inside of four individual 4-inch soufflé dishes, 1¾ inches deep, with softened butter. Put 2½ tablespoons of the sugar in one of the dishes, and rotate it to coat the inside thoroughly. Tip the excess sugar into the next dish, and repeat to coat them all with sugar. Put a baking sheet in the oven and preheat to 350°F.

Pour the milk into a small heavy-based pan. Scrape the seeds from the vanilla bean and add them to the milk with the pod and 1½ tablespoons of the sugar. Bring to a boil.

Put the egg yolks and 2 teaspoons of the sugar in a bowl, and whisk to a ribbon consistency. Add the potato flour, and whisk thoroughly until very smooth. Pour the boiling milk onto the egg mixture, whisking as you go, then return the mixture to the saucepan. Bubble over a low heat for 2 minutes, whisking continuously. Take off the heat, remove the vanilla bean, then add 5 tablespoons of the Grand Marnier. Tip the pastry cream into a bowl and set aside.

Melt 2½ tablespoons of the sugar in a nonstick, heavy-based saucepan over a low heat and cook to a pale, nut-brown caramel. Add the mango pieces and brown them in the caramel for 1 minute. Add the remaining 2 tablespoons Grand Marnier and cook for another minute. Set aside.

To assemble the soufflés, beat the egg whites to soft peaks. Add the remaining sugar and continue to beat until the meringue is firm, but not too stiff. Using a balloon whisk, mix one-third into the pastry cream, then delicately fold in the rest with a spatula.

Divide half the soufflé mixture between the dishes. Spoon in the mango, then fill up the dishes with the rest of the mixture. Smooth the surface with a palette knife, and lightly draw the mixture away from the edge of the dishes with the tip of a small knife. Immediately, place the dishes on the hot baking sheet and bake for about 8 minutes.

To serve, dust the soufflés with a light veil of confectioners' sugar and serve right away, or place them under a hot broiler or salamander for 30 seconds until glazed and caramelized, then serve immediately.

peppermint soufflé in a chocolate crêpe

This flavor combination of dark, bitter chocolate and peppermint liqueur is a chocoholic's delight.

Serves 6
3/4 cup crème pâtissière (page 181)
2 tablespoons peppermint liqueur
4 egg whites (about 2/3 cup)
3 tablespoons sugar
2 ounces good quality bittersweet chocolate, chopped
6 chocolate crêpes (page 61)

To serve:
6 mint sprigs
confectioners' sugar, to dust

Preheat the oven to 400°F. Put the crème pâtissière into a bowl and heat gently in a *bain-marie* or the microwave. Stir in the peppermint liqueur.

Beat the egg whites until soft peaks form, then add the sugar and beat to stiff peaks. Using a whisk, mix a third of the meringue into the flavored crème pâtissière to loosen it. Delicately fold in the rest of the meringue, using a spatula. Scatter the chocolate over the surface and mix in gently.

Lay the crêpes on a large baking sheet. Working quickly and delicately, use a large spoon to pile the soufflé mixture into a dome in the middle of each crêpe. Fold the crêpes over the filling to enclose and immediately place in the hot oven for 3 to 4 minutes.

Take the crêpes out of the oven and lift them onto serving plates with a palette knife. Add the mint sprigs, sprinkle the crêpes with confectioners' sugar, and serve at once.

mousses, terrines, and confits

Mousses and confits require little effort and are relatively easy to prepare. Terrines, however, take time and a degree of organisation ... and there are no short cuts. Don't let this discourage you, as these rustic dishes keep well for several days in the fridge, and their pleasure can extend across several meals. A combination of mousses and terrines is perfect for a buffet, or as an hors d'oeuvre. They give the host a breather before the meal, leaving more time to devote attention to the main dish.

Of the many tempting mousses based on puréed cooked meat or

vegetables, ham mousse (page 69) is one of my favorites. In winter, I often prepare delicate fish or chicken mousses to serve hot, as in my salmon mousse and spinach tartlets (page 70). I sometimes shape these mousses into quenelles, using two tablespoons (see page 69), then poach them in lightly salted water. Creamy and light, they can be coated with hollandaise sauce to make them even more delectable.

The aroma of an eye-catching terrine will make your mouth water, and these appetizing dishes are wonderfully versatile. Vary the lining to suit the different flavors and colors in the terrine; thin strips of fatback, pig's caul, thin crêpes, finely sliced zucchinis, blanched leek, and green cabbage leaves are all suitable. Terrines can be assembled from pork or veal forcemeat, chicken, game, offal, mousses, or small pieces of fish; the possible varieties of color and texture are endless.

I use mainly seasonal ingredients, so my wild mushroom terrine

(page 76), for example, only features on my menus in the fall, when several varieties of wild mushrooms are available. It is important to get the seasoning just right, otherwise the flavor will be disappointing; taste the separate components as you assemble a terrine.

Being the son and grandson of a *charcutier*, confits (food, especially meat, preserved by cooking in its own fat) hold no secrets for me. They are popular in France, especially in the country areas of the south and southwest. Slow-cooked dishes, like *potées* of green cabbage, sarladaise potatoes, and cassoulets benefit from the addition of confit goose, duck, or pork. I never shun them, and I am particularly fond of my original creation of confit rabbit, which I prepare mainly in winter to grill and serve with a salad.

More and more, I am enjoying confit vegetables, such as peppers, eggplant, zucchini, and tomatoes. These have a delicate texture, and should be served as soon as they are ready. I also confit pieces of fish, like chunks of eel or thick salmon fillets, which melt in the mouth.

For fish and meat, I only use fats of the purest quality, taken from the bellies of ducks and geese. These fine fats, available commercially in jars, help to develop the flavors of the main ingredients. For vegetables, I use light olive oil or peanut oil, or clarified butter. Like a court-bouillon, the fat or oil should be flavored with a bouquet garni, some crushed peppercorns, and unpeeled garlic cloves; but don't add salt, as the meat and fish will have already been salted.

I keep confit meats in their fat in the fridge for weeks, so I always have a quick meal on hand – perfect for the holidays or when friends turn up unexpectedly. I can relax, and entertain them with a smile ...

ham mousse with red pepper salsa

This simple, tasty mousse is rustic yet sophisticated – a real gourmet dish. I prefer the texture to be slightly rough, but if you like a creamier mousse, push it through a fine sieve before mixing in the cream. For the best flavor, use a good quality unsmoked ham, cooked on the bone. Prepare the ham mousse a day or two in advance if you like – shape it into quenelles and arrange on the plates 20 minutes before serving.

Serves 8

3 gelatin leaves, or 1 envelope unflavored gelatin
1 1/2 cups velouté sauce made with chicken stock
(page 18, about 1/3 recipe)
1/2 teaspoon paprika
3 1/3 cups whipping cream
14 ounces good quality unsmoked cooked ham, diced
pinch of cayenne pepper
3 tablespoons dry sherry
salt and freshly ground pepper

To serve:

16 small asparagus spears
handful of radicchio and corn salad (mâche)
few drops of lemon juice, to taste
24 hazelnuts, toasted, skinned, and halved
red pepper salsa (page 22)

Soften the gelatin: put the leaves in cold water to cover, or sprinkle powdered gelatin over 2 tablespoons cold water in a small bowl. Slowly heat the velouté sauce until it just reaches a simmer, then take the pan off the heat. Thoroughly drain the gelatin leaves and add them, or the softened powdered gelatin, to the sauce, together with the paprika. Whisk thoroughly until the gelatin has melted. Let cool at room temperature, stirring with a whisk from time to time.

Whip the cream to a ribbon consistency. Put the diced ham into a food processor and whizz for 1 minute, then add the velouté sauce and process for 2 to 3 minutes to make a smooth paste. Transfer to a bowl and place over another bowl containing ice cubes to chill the mixture.

Gently fold the whipped cream into the mixture, using a spatula. Season with salt and cayenne, then gently mix in the sherry; avoid overworking the mousse. Taste and adjust the seasoning with pepper. Scrape the mousse into a dish, cover the surface with plastic wrap to prevent oxidization, and refrigerate.

Take the ham mousse out of the fridge 20 minutes before serving. Peel the ends of the asparagus spears, halve lengthwise and blanch lightly; drain thoroughly. Dress the radicchio and corn salad, simply, with a few drops of lemon juice.

Shape the mousse into quenelles (see below), allowing one or two per person, and place on serving plates. Arrange the radicchio and corn salad, asparagus, and toasted hazelnuts on the plates. Spoon a little red pepper salsa over the ham mousse and accompany with toasted country bread.

SHAPING QUENELLES

Dip two tablespoons into a bowl of warm water to warm them. Scrape one spoon through the mousse towards you to take up an oval quenelle (left). Mold the quenelle onto the second spoon (center), then back onto the first spoon (right) to improve the shape. Place the quenelle on the serving plate.

salmon mousse and spinach tartlets

This simple, yet sophisticated starter is full of wonderful flavors. With the exception of the hollandaise, all the components can be prepared in advance, including the salmon mousse gnocchi. Make the hollandaise just before the meal and serve the extra sauce in a sauceboat.

Serves 6

Tartlet shells:

3/4 pound pâte brisée (page 174, about 3/4 recipe)
flour, to dust

Salmon mousse:

1/2 pound skinless salmon fillet
1 egg white
small pinch of cayenne pepper
1 1/3 cups heavy cream, well chilled
salt

To assemble:

4 tablespoons butter
10 ounces small spinach leaves, washed and stalks removed
pinch of sugar
6 small dill or fennel fronds, plus extra for garnish
1 quantity hollandaise sauce (page 20)

First make the tartlet shells: Lightly flour the work surface and roll out the pastry thinly, 1/16 to 1/8 inch thick. Cut out six 4-inch circles with a pastry cutter and use them to line six 3-inch tartlet molds. Trim off the excess pastry with a small sharp knife. Place the tartlet shells in the fridge and allow to rest for about 20 minutes. Preheat the oven to 400°F.

Prick the tartlet bases with a fork, line with a disk of parchment paper or foil, and fill with dried or ceramic baking beans. Bake for 8 minutes, then remove the beans and paper or foil. Bake for another 2 minutes. Unmold the pastry shells and place on a wire rack.

To prepare the mousse, put the salmon in a food processor and whizz to a smooth purée. Push the salmon purée through a fine sieve into a bowl placed on a bed of crushed ice. Using a wooden spatula, gradually work the egg white into the purée, then season with the cayenne and a little salt. Add the cream, little by little, working it in with the spatula, until you have a slightly firm mousse. Cover the bowl with plastic wrap and refrigerate until ready to use.

Two-thirds fill a shallow 8-inch saucepan with lightly salted water. Bring to a boil and lower the heat so that the water is barely trembling.

To shape the gnocchi, spoon the mousse into a pastry bag fitted with a 3/8-inch plain tip. Twist the end to secure and, using one hand, hold the pastry bag 2 inches above the water. Hold a knife in the other hand.

Apply a consistent, slow pressure to squeeze the mousse from the bag, at the same time stroking the back of the blade over the end of the tip, to cut the emerging mousse into 3/8-inch lengths; allow them to drop into the water. Continue until you have cut half the mousse into gnocchi. Poach them in the barely simmering water for about 2 minutes; they will bob up to the surface when they are cooked.

Using a slotted spoon, transfer them to a bowl of ice water and let cool completely. Prepare and cook the remaining gnocchi in the same way.

Heat the oven to 325°F. Melt the butter in a frying pan over a medium heat. Increase the heat to high, add the spinach with the sugar, and sauté briefly. Season lightly with salt and drain well. Keep warm.

To assemble, warm the pastry shells in the oven for a few minutes. Divide the spinach between them. Plunge the gnocchi into a pan of boiling water for 1 minute to heat them, drain and carefully pile into the pastry shells. Shred the dill or fennel over the gnocchi and coat with hollandaise. Garnish with fennel or dill and serve.

wild boar and morel pâté en croûte

A pear and lime salsa is the perfect foil for this wonderful pâté, which is equally good made with flavorful organic pork, or with pheasant. It will keep in the fridge for up to 5 days.

Serves 8

1 boned shoulder of wild boar or pork (about 1 pound), trimmed of fat and sinews, bones and trimmings reserved
5 ounces veal fillet
7 ounces pork fat
2 tablespoons peanut oil
2 carrots, peeled and chopped
1 onion, peeled and chopped
6 tablespoons dry white wine
1 bouquet garni
3 gelatin leaves, or 1 envelope unflavored gelatin
⁷/₈ cup heavy cream
¹/₂ egg, beaten (about 2 tablespoons)
pinch of cayenne pepper
10 ounces pâte brisée (page 174, about ²/₃ recipe)
flour, to dust
7 ounces fatback, thinly sliced, or unsmoked bacon
2¹/₂ ounces dried morels, soaked in cold water
fine sea salt and freshly ground pepper
1 egg yolk, mixed with 1 tablespoon milk (egg wash)

To serve:

pear and lime salsa (page 23)
pickled baby beets (page 188), optional
pickled plums (page 188), optional

Cut the wild boar, veal, and pork fat into cubes and chill until almost frozen. Meanwhile, make the aspic. Chop the bones. Heat the oil in a frying pan, add the bones, trimmings and sinews, and fry until lightly colored. Add the carrots and onion, fry for 3 minutes, then tip everything into a saucepan. Deglaze the frying pan with the white wine and add to the saucepan. Add cold water to cover the bones generously and bring to a boil. Lower the heat, add the bouquet garni, and simmer gently for 1¹/₂ hours, skimming as necessary.

Soak the gelatin leaves in cold water to cover, or sprinkle the powdered gelatin over 2 tablespoons cold water to soften. Strain the stock through a cheesecloth-lined sieve, slowly so that it remains clear. Squeeze the water from the gelatin leaves, add them, or the softened gelatin, to the stock, and stir until melted. Season with salt and cool until slightly thickened.

To prepare the forcemeat, work the wild boar, veal, and pork fat through the coarse blade of a meat grinder. Mix in the cream, beaten egg, 1¹/₂ teaspoons salt, ¹/₂ teaspoon pepper, and the cayenne, with a spatula.

Roll out the pastry on a lightly floured surface to a 20-inch square, about ³/₁₆ inch thick. Lay the fatback on the pastry, leaving a 2-inch clear border all round. Spread a 1-inch layer of forcemeat over the middle third of the fat. Top with a few morels and cover with another layer of forcemeat. Repeat these layers to use all the forcemeat and morels. Completely enclose the forcemeat with fatback by folding over the overhanging pieces.

Lightly brush the short ends of the pastry with egg wash. Fold one long side over the forcemeat, brush with egg wash, then fold the other long side over the top. Roll out the pastry ends and trim to make 3-inch flaps. Brush lightly with egg wash and fold them up over the pâté. Hold a baking sheet at an angle of 45° against the side of the pâté, then tilt and invert the pâté onto the baking sheet. Refrigerate for 1 hour.

Preheat the oven to 400°F. Brush the pastry with egg wash and lightly score leaves or a lattice pattern with a knife tip. Make two small slits with a knife tip to let steam escape, and cook in the oven for 10 minutes.

Lower the setting to 350°F and cook for another 50 minutes, or until a trussing needle or fine knife tip inserted into the center of the pâté for 10 seconds is hot when withdrawn. If the pastry seems to be over-browning during cooking, cover it with foil.

Using a palette knife, move the pâté to a wire rack and leave for 2 hours or until cold. Insert a small funnel in each opening and pour in the slightly thickened aspic. Refrigerate for 24 hours.

To serve, cut the pâté into slices, with a sharp knife; discard the ends. Put a slice of pâté on each plate and add a spoonful of pear and lime salsa. Accompany with pickled beets and plums, if you like.

wild mushroom terrine

The earthy forest flavors in this terrine are quite astonishing. Depending on availability and cost, you can make the terrine with only two or three varieties of mushroom. It will lose some of its visual impact, but the flavor will still be superb. Use a loaf pan, approximately 8 x 2½ x 2½ inches. This terrine will keep in the fridge for up to 4 days.

Serves 8 to 10

1 pound cèpes or porcini mushrooms (preferably small)
1 1/2 pounds golden chanterelles or girolles
1/2 pound trompettes de la mort (horns of plenty)
1/2 pound oyster mushrooms
1/4 pound enoki mushrooms
6 cups chicken stock (page 16) or vegetable stock (page 17)
5 ounces skinless, boneless chicken breast, finely chopped
3 egg whites
2/3 cup thinly sliced leek
1/3 cup thinly sliced celery
1 small carrot, peeled and cut into thin rings
about 8 gelatin leaves, or 2 envelopes unflavored gelatin
4 herb crêpes (page 58), 11 to 12 inches in diameter
salt and freshly ground white pepper

To serve:

dandelion leaves, or other peppery salad leaves
tarragon leaves
few perfect, small golden chanterelles or girolles, tossed in a light vinaigrette

Using a small knife, cut off the base of the mushrooms and remove any earth, sand, or damaged parts. Halve the trompettes down the middle and check to make sure they are free of sand and grit. Carefully and briefly wash the different mushrooms separately in cold water, then drain well; the enoki won't need washing.

Bring the stock to a boil in a saucepan and cook the different mushrooms, one variety at a time. Allow 5 minutes for cèpes; 4 minutes for chanterelles or girolles; 2 minutes each for trompettes de la mort and oyster mushrooms; 30 seconds for enoki. As soon as they are cooked, lift them out with a slotted spoon and drain in a colander. When all the mushrooms are cooked, boil the stock to reduce it by one third. Let the mushrooms and stock cool.

Set the cèpes aside. Gently press the liquid from the rest of the mushrooms, mix them together and chill.

To clarify the reduced stock, put the chicken, egg whites, and vegetables in a saucepan, mix with a whisk and tip in the cold stock. Bring the mixture to a boil, stirring continuously with the whisk, then turn the heat to very low and simmer gently for 30 minutes. Strain the stock through a fine conical sieve or cheesecloth-lined sieve into a bowl and measure the quantity.

Allow 8 gelatin leaves, or 2 envelopes unflavored gelatin, per 2 cups stock. Soak the gelatin leaves in cold water to cover, or sprinkle powdered gelatin over ¼ cup cold stock (or water) to soften. Squeeze out excess water from the gelatin leaves and add them, or the softened powdered gelatin, to the stock, stirring gently with a spoon until completely dissolved. Leave until cold, then season generously.

To assemble, line the terrine with plastic wrap, letting it overhang the top edge. Trim the crêpes into squares and arrange side-by-side on the plastic wrap to line the dish, leaving plenty of overhang at both ends and one side. Pour in half the cold, liquid aspic, scatter in half the mixed mushrooms (but not the cèpes) and press down gently to embed them in the aspic; they should half-fill the dish. Refrigerate until the aspic starts to set.

Lay the cèpes in a line along the middle of the terrine, then gently pour in the rest of the liquid aspic to ¾ inch from the top. Scatter in the remaining mushrooms and push them lightly into the aspic. Fold the overhanging crêpes over the terrine to enclose it, then fold the plastic wrap over the top; refrigerate for at least 24 hours.

To serve, invert the terrine onto a board, unmold, then carefully peel off the plastic wrap. Using a long, fine-bladed knife dipped in warm water, cut the terrine into slices about ¾ inch thick. Lay a slice on each plate, arrange a few dandelion leaves on one side and strew with tarragon. Arrange the chanterelles alongside.

terrine of baby vegetables

The tiny vegetables in this delicate, flavorsome terrine make it so appealing. Serve it cold or warm with pear and lime salsa (page 23) or a drizzle of olive oil. To warm it, simply slice the terrine and steam for a few minutes. You will need a narrow loaf pan, about 8 x 2½ x 2½ inches.

Serves 8 to 10

Celeriac mousse:

¹/₂ celeriac (celery root), about 10 ounces
2 cups heavy cream
4 eggs
3 egg yolks
salt and freshly ground white pepper

Baby vegetables:

4 ounces baby artichokes (the kind you can eat raw)
3 tablespoons dry white wine
2 tablespoons olive oil
juice of 1 lemon
5 ounces baby carrots, peeled
6 ounces baby fennel
6 to 8 medium asparagus spears
4 ounces baby zucchini
4 ounces broccoli florets
4 herb crêpes (page 58), 11 to 12 inches in diameter

Garnish:

confit tomatoes (page 79)
samphire (salicornia or glasswort)
capers
fennel fronds

First make the celeriac mousse. Peel the celeriac and cut into 1-inch pieces. Place in a saucepan with the cream and cook gently for about 30 minutes, stirring occasionally, until the celeriac is tender and the cream has reduced by half. Tip into a food processor and whizz for 3 minutes, or until smooth. Leave in the processor to cool slightly, until warm. Add the whole eggs, egg yolks, and seasoning and whizz for 1 minute. Turn into a bowl, cover with plastic wrap, and set aside at room temperature.

To prepare the artichokes, cut off the tips of the leaves with a knife and pare the base to leave only the tender part of the stem and heart. Put the artichokes in a saucepan with the white wine, olive oil, lemon juice, and enough water to cover. Cook over a low heat for about 8 minutes until the artichokes are tender and soft. Allow to cool in the liquid, then drain and pat dry; set aside.

Peel, trim, and wash all the other vegetables. Lightly cook them separately in boiling salted water until *al dente*. Plunge into ice water, drain and pat dry.

Preheat the oven to 325°F. To assemble the terrine, line the loaf pan with plastic wrap, letting it overhang all around. Use a knife to trim the crêpes into squares and arrange them side-by-side on the plastic wrap, leaving plenty of overhang at both ends and one side of the loaf pan.

Spread a 1¼-inch layer of cold celeriac mousse over the base. Arrange a line of one variety of vegetable over the mousse and cover with more mousse. Gently tap the terrine to settle it and layer the other vegetables and remaining mousse in the same way, finishing with a 1½-inch layer of mousse. Fold the overhanging crêpes, then the plastic wrap over the top. Stand the terrine in a *bain-marie* and cook in the oven for about 1¼ hours. To check if it is cooked, push a trussing needle or fine knife tip into the center for 10 seconds; it should come out completely clean and feel hot. Let the terrine cool, then refrigerate for at least 24 hours before serving.

To serve, invert the terrine onto a board, unmold and carefully peel off the plastic wrap. Using a fine-bladed knife dipped into warm water, cut into ¾-inch slices. Place on individual plates and garnish with confit tomatoes, some samphire, a few capers, some fennel fronds, and a coarse grinding of white pepper.

confit tomatoes

Confit vegetables are wonderfully versatile. You can serve them alone as tapas, or with toasted country bread, in pasta dishes, salads, or as hors d'oeuvres. To serve them warm, simply heat under a medium broiler or in a saucepan, with a splash of their preserving oil. They can be kept in their oil in the fridge for up to 2 weeks.

Light olive oil is the ideal medium for confit vegetables. Note that olive oil should always be stored away from direct light and used soon after opening, otherwise its flavor is liable to alter and deteriorate.

Confit tomatoes feature in my grilled fillet of lamb with Mediterranean vegetables (page 116).

Makes about 2¼ pounds

2¹/4 pounds very ripe tomatoes (preferably plum), on the stem if possible
1 quart olive oil
2 thyme sprigs
1 bay leaf
2 garlic cloves, peeled and halved
1 teaspoon white peppercorns, crushed
salt

Peel the tomatoes, halve or quarter them, and remove the seeds. Heat the oil in a saucepan until very hot but not smoking, then throw in the tomatoes, thyme, bay leaf, garlic, and pepper. Lower the heat and cook gently at about 160°F (barely scalding) for 15 to 20 minutes, depending on how ripe the tomatoes are.

Allow to cool in the pan, then transfer the tomatoes to a jar. Pour in enough oil to cover them, seal the jar with plastic wrap, and refrigerate until needed. Remove the tomatoes from the oil and season with salt to taste just before serving.

confit sweet peppers

These peppers taste superb if they are grilled over charcoal. If available, I add some vine shoots to enhance the flavor.

Makes about 1¼ pounds

1 pound red, yellow, or green bell peppers
2¹/4 cups olive oil
2 thyme sprigs
1 bay leaf
1 rosemary sprig
1 garlic clove
1 teaspoon white peppercorns, crushed

Using your fingertips, oil the peppers very lightly with a little of the olive oil. Broil under a very high heat (or grill for the best flavor), turning them until the skin blisters and blackens all over.

When the peppers are almost burned, plunge them into a bowl of ice water, then remove and peel them. Halve the peppers lengthwise and remove the white membrane and seeds. Leave them as they are, or cut each half into two.

Heat the oil in a saucepan until very hot, but not smoking. Add the peppers, thyme, bay leaf, rosemary, garlic, and peppercorns. Lower the heat and cook gently at about 160°F for about 30 minutes.

Let the peppers cool in the saucepan, then transfer them to a jar or bowl. Pour in enough oil to cover them, seal the jar with plastic wrap, and keep in the fridge until ready to use.

confit garlic

Use these sweet garlic cloves as a garnish for roast or grilled chicken and lamb, toss into cooked pasta, or smear on warm toast and sprinkle with pepper.

Makes about 1¼ pounds
1 pound new season's garlic
2 cups olive oil
1 rosemary sprig
1 bay leaf
1 teaspoon coriander seeds

Peel the garlic, or leave unpeeled if you prefer. Heat the oil in a saucepan until very hot but not smoking, then add the other ingredients. Lower the heat and cook gently at about 160°F for 10 minutes if the garlic is peeled, 15 minutes if not.

Let the garlic cool in the saucepan, then transfer it to a jar. Pour in enough olive oil to cover, then cover the jar with plastic wrap, and refrigerate until ready to use.

rabbit confit

I prepare confits with all kinds of meat and poultry, from duck legs to pieces of pork or lamb shoulder, poultry gizzards, whole quail, and squab pigeon. The method is always the same. You just need to adjust the salting and cooking times according to the size of the ingredient.

It is always handy to have a confit in the fridge, ready to grill or roast (depending on the variety) for impromptu entertaining. I often serve a confit with shredded cavolo nero, stir-fried until crunchy and scattered over lentils. The combination of crisp cabbage, tender lentils, and rich confit is sheer perfection. And do try my grilled confit of rabbit and apples with walnuts (page 123), illustrated opposite.

Serves 4
4 rabbit legs
4 rabbit shoulders
6 tablespoons coarse cooking salt or kosher salt
4 thyme sprigs
2 bay leaves
3 pounds duck fat, or 6½ cups olive oil
1 tablespoon crushed white peppercorns, 1 thyme sprig and 2 bay leaves, tied in a piece of cheesecloth

Using your fingertips, rub the salt firmly into the rabbit legs for about 3 minutes and the shoulders for about 2 minutes. Closely pack all the rabbit pieces into a deep dish, adding the thyme sprigs and bay leaves. Cover with plastic wrap and refrigerate for 30 minutes, then take out the shoulders, leaving the legs for another 15 minutes. Rinse the shoulders under a trickle of cold water and pat them dry with a dish towel. Do the same with the legs.

Heat the duck fat or olive oil to 160°F in a flameproof casserole or roasting pan and add the bag of herbs and peppercorns. Plunge in the rabbit legs and cook for 15 minutes, then add the shoulders. Cook for another 30 minutes, keeping the temperature at a constant 160°F. Turn off the heat and let the rabbit cool in the fat or oil at room temperature for at least 2 hours.

Using kitchen tongs or a fork, carefully transfer the rabbit pieces to a bowl or deep dish. Strain the cooking fat or oil through a conical sieve onto the rabbit pieces. Cover with plastic wrap and refrigerate.

This confit will keep in the fridge for up to a couple of weeks. It can be served either roasted or grilled. Simply remove the fat from the rabbit pieces before you cook them.

pasta, grains, and rice

Pasta has been part of my repertoire ever since I began cooking. I love making ravioli filled with tender vegetables, ricotta, and raisins; fish and seafood (notably lobster); chicken mousse or meat. To make a change, I flavor and color the pasta, and make cappelletti. I fill these with wild mushrooms and serve them with herb salsa (page 88), or a purée of Jerusalem artichokes or carrots with cilantro. In the fall, I tint the pasta red with beet juice; in winter, I use black squid or cuttlefish ink; in summer, yellow saffron infused in water; and in spring, I layer

flat-leaf parsley, basil, tarragon, or fennel fronds between two thin sheets of pasta to give a delicate green, herb-flavored marbling – a reflection of nature on the plate.

When entertaining on a large scale, I cook my pasta *al dente* beforehand, refresh, drain, and toss it in a little peanut oil, then spread it on a plate, cover with plastic wrap, and refrigerate. When ready to serve, I reheat it in boiling water for 30 seconds, drain, and toss it in melted butter or olive oil. Pasta is equally delicious served cold with a salsa or vinaigrette, or mixed with a little mayonnaise (page 20).

The best rice I have tasted on my travels has been in Vietnam and Italy. I use varieties from all over the world, choosing them to complement my recipes. Thai jasmine rice must be rinsed in cold water before cooking; I then fold it in a muslin cloth and cook it in a steamer for 30 minutes, stirring with a kitchen fork every 10 minutes to aerate it.

Basmati rice must be soaked in cold water for 20 minutes before using; this helps it to absorb the cooking water. Basmati is a good balance for spicy dishes, as its neutral taste absorbs the flavors. It is delicious cooked with a touch of grated fresh ginger and lemon grass.

I like to use carnaroli rice for my seafood risotto with crustacean essence (page 94). A risotto is like a soufflé – it won't wait for your guests, so they must wait for it. Round-grain arborio rice makes a good creamy rice pudding, to serve with poached cherries (page 106).

Whatever the dish, note that it is not wise to reheat rice, as this can activate a harmful bacteria, *bacillus cereus,* which is sometimes present in all varieties. If you must reheat rice, then do so shortly after cooking and make sure that it is boiling hot.

I often serve grain-based dishes – such as couscous, polenta, and tabbouleh – on their own, enhancing their flavor and appearance with delicate ingredients like fresh herbs, grated cheese, seafood, and baby vegetables. For a couscous *garni* (which I like very spicy), I vary the meats and vegetables according to the season. As it is an abundant dish, I never serve a first course beforehand; just a light, refreshing lime-scented mint sorbet afterwards.

In summer, I mix my tabbouleh with cold lobster or *langoustine* tails and confit tomatoes; redolent with lemon and parsley, this refreshing dish has a strong Mediterranean influence.

In winter, I cook polenta in hot chicken stock or milk to a soft purée consistency, then off the heat, I add egg yolks, grated Parmesan, and sautéed sliced cèpes. When cold, I form it into cakes, fry these in a little olive oil, and serve with roast or pan-fried pheasant ... delicious!

pasta dough

This recipe is meant for 4 people, but no doubt some will find it just enough for one. The dough is very malleable and is perfect for cappelletti, ravioli, and all filled pasta. You can make it in a food processor, but you must be careful to avoid overworking the mixture.

Serves 4

3 egg yolks
1¹/₂ whole eggs
2 teaspoons olive oil
2 teaspoons cold water
¹/₂ teaspoon fine salt
1³/₄ cups Italian "tipo 00" flour, or all-purpose flour

Put all the ingredients, except the flour, in a bowl and mix lightly with a fork.

Tip the flour into a large bowl, make a well in the middle, and add the liquid mixture. Use the fingertips of one hand to mix the wet ingredients, gradually drawing in the flour with the other hand, until it is all incorporated and you have a homogeneous dough.

Turn the dough onto a floured surface and sprinkle with flour. Knead and stretch the dough 3 or 4 times with the palm of your hand until it is pliable. Roll it into a ball, wrap in plastic wrap, and let rest in the fridge for 1 hour.

green olive pasta

The taste of green olives in this unusual pasta is so pleasant that I always serve myself a very generous portion, which I sauce with just a drizzle of extra virgin olive oil. The dough is softer than the plain version and cooks very quickly, so it will be perfectly *al dente* in just a few minutes.

Serves 6

1 whole egg
2 egg yolks
2 teaspoons olive oil
3¹/₂ ounces green olives, pitted, patted dry, and very finely chopped
¹/₂ teaspoon fine salt
2¹/₈ cups Italian "tipo 00" flour, or all-purpose flour

Put the egg, egg yolks, olive oil, olives, and salt in a bowl and mix lightly with a fork.

Tip the flour into a large bowl, make a well in the middle, and add the olive mixture. Use the fingertips of one hand to mix the wet ingredients, gradually drawing in the flour with the other hand, until it is all incorporated and you have a homogeneous dough.

Turn the dough onto a floured surface and sprinkle with flour. Knead and stretch the dough 3 or 4 times with the palm of your hand, then roll it into a ball. Wrap in plastic wrap and allow to rest in the fridge for 1 hour.

ROLLING AND SHAPING PASTA

Roll out the dough in manageable quantities, keeping the rest wrapped in plastic wrap to stop it drying out. Pass it through the pasta machine on the widest setting, then repeat, reducing the setting by one notch each time, until the pasta is about $\frac{1}{16}$ inch thick.

Once you have reached the required thickness, pass the dough through the pasta machine a second time on the same setting – this helps to prevent the pasta from shrinking as you cut it.

Fit the appropriate cutter to the machine and pass the pasta through to cut your desired shape – tagliatelle, fettuccine, spaghetti, or what you will.

If you are making shaped pasta, such as cappelletti (page 89), you should use the sheets of dough as soon as you have rolled them.

Alternatively you can, of course, roll and shape pasta the old-fashioned way, using a rolling pin and cutting it with a knife.

serving suggestions

• Toss plain pasta with seared cherry tomatoes flavored with thyme flowers, and flakes of drained, canned tuna in olive oil.

• Try serving warm baby vegetables cooked à la grecque (see page 51) with olive pasta.

• Slices of grilled, very spicy sausage added to red pepper salsa (page 22) complement the flavor of my green olive pasta perfectly.

fettuccine with smoked mussels and pesto

You can smoke the mussels for this elegant pasta dish several hours in advance. Simply keep them in the fridge, covered with plastic wrap so that they don't dry out. Steam for a few minutes just before serving. These quantities are appropriate for a starter, light lunch, or supper. Increase the quantities to serve as a substantial main course. (Illustrated on page 46.)

Serves 4

2¹/4 pounds lightly smoked mussels (page 47)
14 ounces fettuccine, freshly made from 1 quantity
pasta dough (page 84), or bought fresh pasta
4 tablespoons olive oil
juice of 1 lemon
¹/2 quantity pesto (page 25)
salt and freshly ground pepper
4 basil sprigs, preferably purple, to garnish

Shell most of the mussels, keeping a few in their half-shell for garnish.

Bring a saucepan of salted water to a boil. Add the fettuccine with 2 tablespoons olive oil and cook for 3 to 4 minutes, until *al dente*. Drain and return to the pan. Add the remaining olive oil and the lemon juice. Season with pepper to taste, add the shelled mussels, and toss lightly.

Immediately divide the fettuccine and mussels between 4 deep plates or shallow bowls. Arrange the reserved mussels on top, add a generous drizzle of pesto, and put a basil sprig on the edge of each bowl.

wild mushroom cappelletti with herb salsa

I think of cappelletti as little cushions of happiness. I could eat them forever and they fully justify the time they take to make. Instead of a mixture of mushrooms, you could use just one flavorful variety, like cèpes or morels.

When artichokes are in season, I include some cooked, finely diced artichoke hearts for a pleasant, nutty taste. In winter, I fill cappelletti with finely puréed Jerusalem artichokes or pumpkin purée flavored with curry spices and a few finely snipped cilantro leaves. Use these "little peaked hats" as a vehicle of discovery and let your imagination run riot …

Serves 6

1 pound pasta dough (page 84)

Filling:

1¹/4 pounds wild mushrooms (girolles, chanterelles, cèpes, horns of plenty, etc., in equal amounts)
4 tablespoons clarified butter (page 188)
¹/2 cup chopped shallots
¹/2 cup chopped flat-leaf parsley
salt and freshly ground pepper

To assemble and serve:

2 egg yolks, mixed with 2 tablespoons milk
(egg wash)
flour, to dust
2 tablespoons peanut oil
1 quantity herb salsa (page 24)
12 flat-leaf parsley sprigs, to garnish

To make the filling, cut off the base of the mushroom stalks and any earthy, gritty, or damaged parts, using a small, sharp knife. Halve the horns of plenty down the middle and make sure they are free of debris or sand. If necessary, delicately and very briefly wash the different mushroom varieties separately in cold water and drain, or simply wipe them gently with a damp cloth. Chop the different varieties, keeping them separate.

Heat the clarified butter in a frying pan over a medium heat and put in the girolles and chanterelles. When they have exuded their liquid, add the horns of plenty and finally the cèpes. Sauté briskly until all the liquid has evaporated. Add the shallots and cook for another minute. Scatter on the chopped parsley and season with salt and pepper. Set aside, while you roll out and cut the pasta.

Divide the pasta dough in half; keep one portion tightly wrapped. Roll the other half through the pasta machine into a long sheet, 1/16 inch thick and about 4 inches wide. Delicately brush off any excess flour. Using a large cook's knife, trim the edges to ensure a consistent width of 4 inches, then cut into nine 4-inch squares. Fill and shape to make cappelletti (see right), then place on a lightly floured dish towel. Repeat with the rest of the pasta to make 18 cappelletti in total.

To cook the cappelletti, bring a pan of lightly salted water to a boil and add the peanut oil. Gently put in the cappelletti, lower the heat to simmering point, and cook for 5 to 6 minutes, until *al dente*.

To serve, lift the cappelletti out of the water with a slotted spoon, drain, and place three on each warmed plate. Spoon a little herb salsa over each cappelletti, garnish with parsley sprigs, and serve at once.

SHAPING CAPPELLETTI

Brush two adjacent sides of each square very lightly with egg wash.

Put a tablespoon of filling towards that corner, but stop just short of the line of the egg wash.

Fold the opposite corner onto the egg washed corner to make a triangle, and press very lightly to seal the edges.

Trim the edges to neaten, then cut off the two points which form the base of the triangle.

Dab a little egg wash onto one of the cut ends and, stretching them gently, fold them up and over until the two points meet. Slide your index finger between the base of the cappelletti and the two sides, pressing them firmly between your thumb and index finger to seal them tightly.

guinea fowl and lamb couscous

I was introduced to couscous by Chougui, an Algerian cook, whose couscous was second to none. I like to use guinea fowl rather than the more traditional chicken. Sometimes I make it with pheasants, which are inexpensive and tasty, cooking the breasts for no more than 20 minutes, to keep them moist. The best accompaniment to this great winter dish is a glass of ice-cold water.

Serves 6

1¹/₄ pounds carrots, peeled and sliced into thick
rounds

12 baby turnips, peeled

14 ounces pumpkin, peeled, seeded, and cut into
6 chunks

14 ounces zucchini, cut into almond shapes

¹/₂ white cabbage, halved

¹/₃ cup dried chickpeas, soaked in cold water for
24 hours and drained

²/₃ cup currants or raisins, soaked in hot water for
30 minutes and drained

1 guinea fowl, about 3¹/₄ pounds

1 shoulder of lamb, about 4¹/₂ pounds, boned and
trimmed of all fat and sinews

²/₃ cup peanut oil

10 ounces onions, peeled and cut into chunks

2 pounds tomatoes, peeled, seeded, and cut
into chunks

2 teaspoons sweet paprika

1 large bouquet garni, including 2 celery stalks

salt and freshly ground pepper

Couscous:

2 cups medium-coarse couscous

1¹/₄ cups warm water

To serve:

coriander (cilantro) sprigs

3 tablespoons pumpkin seeds, toasted

3 tablespoons harissa paste

Tie the carrots, turnips, pumpkin, and zucchini in separate pieces of cheesecloth, securing with long lengths of string. Tie each piece of cabbage in cheesecloth and blanch in boiling water for 2 minutes.

Drain the chickpeas, put them in a saucepan, cover with cold water, and bring to a boil. Immediately lower the heat and simmer gently for 2 hours. Drain, rinse in cold water, drain well, and add to the currants.

Cut the guinea fowl into 6 pieces and the lamb into 1¹/₄-inch cubes; season both with salt. Heat 2 tablespoons oil in a large frying pan and fry the guinea fowl pieces to an appetizing golden brown. Transfer to a plate and keep covered. Heat another 2 tablespoons oil in the pan, sear the lamb, and fry until browned; transfer to a flameproof casserole or large saucepan.

Pour off the fat from the frying pan, add another 2 tablespoons oil, and brown the onions gently. Add to the lamb. Put the tomatoes and paprika in the frying pan and cook gently for 5 minutes. Add to the casserole, then pour in cold water to cover generously. Bring to a boil over a high heat. Skim the surface and lower the heat to a bare simmer. Add the bouquet garni, cover, and cook for 1 hour, skimming as necessary.

Add the guinea fowl thighs and legs, carrots, and cabbage; cook for another 55 minutes. Now add the guinea fowl breast pieces, the turnips, zucchini, and pumpkin and cook for another 20 minutes.

Put the couscous in a bowl. Sprinkle on the warm water, while stirring the couscous with your fingertips. Leave to absorb the water for 4 to 5 minutes. Moisten with 4 tablespoons oil, stirring with your fingertips to aerate the couscous, and salt lightly. Add the chickpeas and currants and transfer to the top of a steamer.

Put 2 large ladlefuls of the cooking liquid from the meat into the base of the steamer and steam the couscous over a medium heat for 30 minutes, stirring it with a fork every 10 minutes to ensure the grains cook evenly and don't stick together.

To serve, combine the meat and vegetables in a warmed bowl, pour over the cooking liquid and scatter with coriander. Pile the couscous into another warmed dish and sprinkle with pumpkin seeds. Dilute the harissa in 3 tablespoonfuls cooking liquid and serve separately, to allow guests to spice up their couscous as they wish.

tabbouleh

Here is an innovative way to serve this popular Middle Eastern dish, which I adore making, especially when I am in Provence. Like risotto, there are countless versions; my favorite is intensely lemony and full of fresh parsley and mint. It tastes even better the day after it is made.

Serves 6

2 cups medium or coarse bulgur wheat
2¹/4 cups cold water
³/4 pound very firm, ripe tomatoes
³/4 pound cucumber
6 small scallions, including tender green leaves, finely snipped
3 tablespoons chopped curly parsley
¹/2 cup snipped mint leaves
6 tablespoons olive oil
juice of 3 lemons
12 black olives, pitted and sliced
salt and freshly ground pepper

Garnish:

1 green bell pepper
6 inner Savoy cabbage leaves
2 limes, cut into wedges, plus 6 lime segments
6 mint sprigs, plus a handful of shredded mint
6 flat-leaf parsley sprigs
4 tablespoons chopped curly parsley

Put the bulgur wheat in a saucepan, add the water, and bring to a boil over a medium heat, stirring occasionally. Cook for 10 minutes, then tip into a sieve, refresh under cold water for 30 seconds to stop the cooking, and let drain thoroughly for 30 minutes.

Meanwhile, seed and finely dice the tomatoes. Peel and finely dice the cucumber. Sprinkle with salt, leave for 5 minutes, then drain and pat dry.

Tip the bulgur wheat onto a dish towel, roll it in the towel to dry thoroughly, then place in a salad bowl. Add all the other ingredients and mix gently, seasoning to taste. Cover with plastic wrap and leave in a cool place for at least 2 hours to let the flavors develop.

To serve, peel the green pepper with a swivel peeler, then pare long, fine slices with the peeler. Line individual dishes with the cabbage leaves. Divide the tabbouleh between them, heaping it into a dome and arranging a few of the olive slices on the surface. Garnish each serving with green pepper strips, a lime segment, and a little shredded mint.

Provide each guest with a dish containing a lime wedge, mint and parsley sprigs, and some chopped parsley, so they can flavor their tabbouleh to taste.

rice pilaf

I serve this pilaf as an accompaniment to my lobster fricassée with peppers (page 144), flavoring it with curry spices, a few toasted pine nuts and blanched golden raisins. Flavored with herbs rather than spices, it is delicious with steamed fish, such as my fillets of sea bass in green jackets (page 99). To serve the pilaf as a tasty starter, I add some sautéed chicken livers and sliced button mushrooms at the last moment.

Serves 4

4 tablespoons butter
¹/2 cup finely chopped onion
1 cup long-grain rice
1²/3 cups boiling water
1 thyme or rosemary sprig, or 1 tablespoon ground curry spices (cumin, coriander, turmeric, etc.)
salt and freshly ground pepper

Preheat the oven to 400°F. Melt the butter in a flameproof casserole, add the onion and sweat it gently for 1 minute. Add the rice, increase the heat very slightly, and cook for about 2 minutes, stirring with a wooden spoon, until the rice becomes translucent.

Pour on the boiling water, add your chosen herb or spices, and season sparingly with salt. Cover and cook in the oven for 18 minutes.

Let the pilaf rest, still covered, in a warm place for 8 to 10 minutes. Discard the herb, fork through the rice, season to taste, and serve.

seafood risotto with crustacean essence

The correct way to make a risotto is a subject of debate among Italians – should you or should you not stir the rice as it cooks; must you use a wooden spoon? My only concern is to make a good risotto and this method works for me. Here calendulas give the rice a pale golden tint, which complements the prawns and squid perfectly, but they are not essential.

Serves 6

Risotto:

3¹/₃ cups fish stock (page 16)
6 tablespoons butter
¹/₂ cup finely chopped onions
1 cup risotto rice, preferably carnaroli
6 tablespoons dry white wine
2 edible calendula flowers (optional)
1¹/₂ ounces Parmesan cheese, freshly grated
salt and freshly ground pepper

Seafood, and crustacean essence:

18 large raw shrimp in shell, with heads if possible
⁷/₈ cup cold fish stock (page 16)
24 baby squid, preferably fresh, cleaned
2 tablespoons olive oil
2 teaspoons butter

First make the risotto. Bring the fish stock to a boil in a saucepan and keep it at a simmer.

Melt 4 tablespoons of the butter in a small saucepan, add the onions, and sweat gently for 2 minutes, then add the rice and stir with a spoon.

Increase the heat slightly and continue stirring until the rice turns opaque and begins to "sing."

Pour in the wine, stir once only, then allow to cook until two-thirds of the liquid has evaporated.

Add two-thirds of the hot fish stock and a little salt. Stir once only and allow to cook gently for about 12 minutes, adding a little more hot stock if necessary.

Check the texture of the rice; it should be very firm, almost crunchy. Add the rest of the stock and cook for another 2 to 3 minutes.

Take the pan off the heat, add the calendula petals, if using, sprinkle in the Parmesan, and stir in the remaining butter. Cover the pan with a lid and let stand off the heat for 6 to 8 minutes.

Put the shrimp in a saucepan, cover with the cold fish stock, and bring to a boil. Immediately take the pan off the heat and add the squid. Cover the pan and let stand for 3 minutes.

Drain the seafood, reserving the stock; keep the squid warm. Shell the shrimp, reserving the heads (or shells, if headless), and add to the squid.

To make the crustacean essence, crush the shrimp heads (or shells) with the flat of a large knife. Put them in a small saucepan with the olive oil and color over a high heat for 3 or 4 minutes. Add the reserved fish stock and whizz in a food processor for 3 minutes. Strain through a fine conical sieve or cheesecloth-lined sieve set over a small saucepan. Reduce the resulting liquid to a slightly syrupy consistency. Remove from the heat and whisk in the butter.

Mix two-thirds of the shrimp and squid into the rice. Divide between deep serving plates and arrange the rest of the seafood on top. Drizzle with a few drops of the reduction to serve.

steamed and poached dishes

Over the past decade, steaming has become one of my favorite cooking methods. It is extremely quick, and preserves the vitamins, colors, and flavors of the ingredients better than any other form of cooking. It is ideal for preparing a light, healthy, digestible meal. You can either use a steamer or saucepan with a Chinese-style wooden steaming insert, flavoring the water in the pan with herbs and wine, or spices; or use a light stock. Apply salt directly to the food, rather than add it to the liquid.

One of my favorite dishes is my steamed poussins scented with ginger and lemon grass (page 100). These take very little time to cook, and I find the perfumed flavors of this utterly simple dish extremely seductive. Steamed rice makes the perfect accompaniment.

Green vegetables, especially asparagus, taste better and retain their qualities perfectly when they are steamed. My little steamed stuffed cabbages (page 99) can be prepared in advance, and need only 8 minutes cooking at the last moment. I even use steam to peel tomatoes and peaches; it takes only a few seconds and even preserves the flavor and color of very ripe fruit.

Poaching is a delicate method of cooking. The temperature of the poaching liquid (water, court bouillon, wine, milk, sugar syrup, etc.) must always be kept at between 150°F and 175°F. It is essential to obey this rule so as not to destroy the proteins of the ingredient you are poaching, so use a cooking thermometer.

Steaming makes fish more succulent and preserves their texture and intrinsic flavors. It is more suitable for pieces or fillets than whole fish. I often wrap the pieces in spinach or other leaves to protect them from the heat and seal in the flavors, as in my steamed fillets of sea bass in green jackets (page 99), for example. The only minus point is that, unlike poaching, you cannot use the liquid as the base for a sauce.

I like to add dulse seaweed to the steamer for a couple of minutes just before serving steamed fish. I love its tender texture, mild flavor and attractive red coloring, which are all preserved by the last minute cooking. When steaming a 1 pound-lobster, I embed it in a nest of seaweed, so that during the 10 minutes or so it takes to cook, it absorbs the iodine flavor of the seaweed. It needs no other accompaniment than a vegetable *nage* (page 17).

Fish are equally good poached whole or in pieces. A whole poached trout *au bleu* occasionally appears as a speciality on my menu at The Waterside Inn. For my turbot poached in red wine (page 101), I use steaks; the outer part of the flesh is tinted by the red wine, while the center remains white and firm-textured.

Most fruits are suitable for poaching. Vary the poaching liquid according to the texture of the fruit, using sugar syrup, sweet wine, or water, and adding an appropriate herb or spice; rosemary, lavende,r mint, or cloves, for example. Or, for something out of the ordinary, you could use a flavored tea, as I do in my poached apricots in assam tea syrup (page 111).

steamed fillets of sea bass in green jackets

This lovely, light dish is ideal for entertaining when time is short, since both the sauce and the fish can be prepared in advance. Simply reheat the coulis in a *bain-marie* and steam the sea bass 10 minutes before serving. You can use spinach leaves to wrap the fish, but lettuce has a more delicate texture and flavor, which complements the sea bass better. Rice pilaf flavored with herbs (page 93) and cauliflower purée are unusual and delicious accompaniments.

Serves 4

4 portions of sea bass, about 6 ounces each (cut from a good thick fillet from a 5¹/2-pound fish)
8 attractive dark green outer lettuce leaves
salt and freshly ground pepper

To serve:

2 tablespoons clarified butter (page 188)
shredded white part of 2 leeks, deep-fried
leek coulis with saffron and dill (page 27)

Remove the skin and season the fish with salt and pepper. Blanch the lettuce leaves and refresh, then drain. Wrap each sea bass portion in 2 lettuce leaves, then wrap each parcel in plastic wrap.

Half-fill a steamer with water, and salt lightly. Bring to a boil, then lower the heat so that the water barely trembles. Put in the steaming rack, arrange the sea bass parcels inside, cover, and steam for 8 to 10 minutes. To test whether the fish is done, insert a trussing needle or fine knife tip into the center for 10 seconds; it should penetrate easily and feel hot when you remove it and place it on your inner arm.

To serve, carefully peel off the plastic wrap from the fish parcels. Place one on each plate and brush with clarified butter. Make a little airy pile of deep-fried leek on top of each parcel and pour the leek coulis around the edge. Serve at once.

little steamed stuffed cabbages

Serve these cabbages as they are, brushed lightly with melted butter, or with leek coulis with saffron and dill (page 27). They go well with my roast stuffed festive goose (page 129). Prepare ahead if you like and chill until ready to steam.

Serves 6

2 potatoes (preferably Desirée), 10 ounces total weight
7 ounces butter, clarified (page 188)
1 thyme sprig
1 head of broccoli, cut into florets and blanched
12 small Brussels sprouts, trimmed
1 medium Savoy cabbage, outer leaves removed
salt and freshly ground pepper

Peel the potatoes and cut into ¹/2-inch dice. Rinse and dry in a cloth. Heat the clarified butter in a saucepan over a medium heat, add the potatoes with the thyme, and cook until just tender. Drain and put in a bowl with the broccoli. Season to taste.

Cook the Brussels sprouts in boiling salted water until tender. Refresh, drain, and season. Put in a bowl.

Take off the cabbage leaves and blanch in boiling salted water for a few minutes. Refresh, drain, and cut out the thickest part of the ribs if necessary.

To assemble the cabbages, place a double thickness of plastic wrap, about 6 inches square, on the work surface. Lay a cabbage leaf on it, season, and place a generous tablespoon of potato and broccoli mixture in the middle, then add 2 Brussels sprouts.

Fold the cabbage leaf over the stuffing to enclose it. Bring the 4 corners of the plastic wrap together over the cabbage, turn over to enclose the cabbage ball tightly and knot the excess wrap to preserve the cabbage shape. Make 5 more "cabbages" in this way.

Fill a steamer pan with water, salt lightly, cover, and bring to a boil. Put the stuffed cabbages in the top of the steamer, cover, and steam for 8 minutes.

Lift out onto a plate, cut the plastic wrap knots, and gently invert the cabbages onto a serving platter, peeling off the plastic wrap. Serve at once.

steamed poussins scented with ginger and lemongrass

On a recent visit to Thailand, one of my former chefs, Marco Avitabilé (who now oversees the kitchens at the Grand Hyatt in Hong Kong) prepared a delicious chicken for me along the lines of this recipe. I have used poussin or baby chicken, and added a few variations of my own. The bouillon adds a peasant touch, which I adore. This dish should be eaten piping hot.

Serves 4

1 1/2 quarts water
3/4 ounce fresh ginger, peeled and thinly sliced
2 lemongrass stalks, cut lengthwise into thick julienne
2 poussins or squab chickens, 12 to 14 ounces each, wishbones removed
1/2 pound broccoli florets
1 tablespoon cornstarch, mixed with 2 tablespoons cold water
2 tablespoons peanut oil
oil for deep-frying
1 1/2 cups arugula leaves
salt and freshly ground pepper

To serve:

1 cup fragrant Thai long-grain rice, freshly steamed

Put the water into the steamer pan, salt very lightly, cover, and bring to a boil. Meanwhile, mix the ginger with the lemongrass and place inside the poussins; they don't need trussing. Put them in the top of the steamer, cover, and steam for 15 to 20 minutes.

Scatter over the broccoli florets, and cook for another 2 minutes. Transfer the broccoli to a bowl, cover with plastic wrap, and keep warm. Cut off the legs and breasts from the poussins; wrap the breasts in foil and let rest in a warm place. Reserve the legs.

Break up the carcasses and put them in the cooking water in the base of the steamer, together with the ginger and lemongrass mixture (from inside the poussins). Simmer for 5 minutes, add the blended cornstarch, and cook, stirring, for 1 minute, then strain through a fine sieve into a saucepan. Adjust the seasoning, if necessary; keep the sauce warm.

Heat the peanut oil in a frying pan. Add the poussin legs, skin-side down, and fry over a medium heat until the skin is slightly crunchy and a beautiful light golden brown.

Heat the oil for deep-frying in a suitable pan to about 325ºF. Make sure the arugula is completely dry. Put it into the hot oil and deep-fry until very crisp, as you would parsley, stirring with a slotted spoon. Lift out of the oil with the slotted spoon and drain on paper towels. If the arugula isn't as crisp as it should be, reheat the oil and fry it for another 2 to 3 minutes. Drain on paper towels and salt lightly.

To serve, pile the hot rice into a dome on a serving platter and arrange the poussin breasts and legs on top. Scatter on little heaps of broccoli and arugula, and serve the sauce separately.

turbot poached in red wine

Turbot, the "king of fish," is always best cooked on the bone, with its skin. My friend André Charial makes this powerful red wine sauce with Château de Romanin at the famous Ostau de Beaumanière. Its deep red color contrasts superbly with the whiteness of the turbot, and it enhances the depth of flavor. If turbot seems too expensive, brill is an excellent alternative.

Serves 4

4 turbot steaks on the bone, with skin, about
10 ounces each
16 small new potatoes
1/2 lemon
1 bottle red wine (e.g., Côtes du Rhône)
5 tablespoons fish stock (page 16)
4 tablespoons butter
salt and freshly ground pepper

Sauce:

1 cup Château de Romanin, or Côtes du Rhône
1/4 cup thinly sliced shallot
1/4 cup thinly sliced button mushrooms
7/8 cup veal stock, chicken stock (page 16), or
vegetable stock (page 17)

Garnish:

4 deep-fried, tender sage sprigs

Season the turbot steaks lightly with salt and pepper; set aside.

Using a small sharp knife, pare the potatoes into mushroom shapes: make a 1⁄4-inch horizontal cut around the circumference, about one-third down the length of each potato, to form the mushroom cap, then cut away the excess potato to shape the stalk (see photograph, above right). Put the potato "mushrooms" in a pan of lightly salted water, add the lemon (to prevent the potato disintegrating), and cook until tender. Leave the potatoes in the cooking water.

To make the sauce, pour the Château de Romanin into a small saucepan, add the shallot and mushrooms, and reduce by two-thirds over a low heat. Add the stock and reduce again until the sauce lightly coats the back of a spoon. Strain the sauce through a fine conical sieve, season with salt and pepper, and keep warm.

To poach the fish, put the turbot steaks, Côtes du Rhône, and fish stock in a wide shallow saucepan and set over a medium heat. As soon as the liquid starts to bubble, lower the heat to a bare simmer, no more than 175˚F, and skim off any scum from the surface. Poach the fish for 15 minutes. To test whether it is cooked, insert a trussing needle or fine knife tip into the flesh for 10 seconds; it should penetrate easily and feel hot when you take it out. Lift out the turbot steaks and carefully remove the dark and white skin with a knife tip.

To serve, melt the butter, drain the potato "mushrooms", and roll them in the butter. Divide the potatoes between the plates. Place a turbot steak on each plate with a fried sage sprig to one side. Spoon a little sauce over the turbot and serve the rest of the sauce in a sauce boat.

OPENING OYSTERS

Hold the oyster in the palm of one hand, using a cloth for protection. Hold an oyster knife in the other hand and push the tip of the blade into the pointed end of the oyster.

Slide the blade all along the inner edge of the top shell so as to sever the muscle that joins the two shells.

Lift off the top shell, leaving the oyster in the lower shell.

Carefully release the oyster from the cupped shell and slide it into a bowl with its juices. Make sure you pick out any loose bits of shell. Rinse the cupped shells in cold water and reserve for serving the oysters.

poached oysters with mayonnaise and horseradish

Oysters poached like this are full of flavor, which is further accentuated by the mustardy mayonnaise and grated horseradish. Fresh-tasting watercress makes this dish easy on the palate. If you prefer, you can use flat native oysters, but I find them too rich and fatty. As with all shellfish, it is essential to use only the freshest oysters and to eat them within an hour of preparing the dish.

Serves 4

24 medium (size 2) oysters, opened
3^1/$_2$ tablespoons dry white wine
1 pound watercress
1^1/$_4$ cups mustardy mayonnaise (page 20)
2 tablespoons grated horseradish, preferably fresh
about 72 tiny tarragon sprigs
salt and freshly ground pepper
coarse sea salt, to serve

Tip the oysters and their juices into a saucepan, pour in the white wine and set over a medium heat. As soon as the liquid comes up to a gentle simmer, no more than 175°F, turn off the heat. The oysters will be poached in about 15 seconds. Keep them in their juices at room temperature.

Pick the leaves off the watercress, shred them, and mix with ½ cup of the mayonnaise. Season to taste.

To serve, divide the watercress mayonnaise between the cupped oyster shells. Drain the oysters and place them on a dish towel to dry for a few seconds. Put an oyster in each shell and season with half a turn of the pepper mill.

Coat the oysters with a little mayonnaise, leaving a border of watercress showing. Scatter a little grated horseradish over each oyster and lay 3 tarragon sprigs on top. Serve on a bed of coarse sea salt; this not only looks good, but holds the oysters steady.

poached cherries with creamy rice pudding

I often poach cherries in Banyuls, a strong, sweet red wine from the Roussillon region, which is served as an apéritif. I love to serve these poached cherries on rice pudding, scattered with very fine shreds of tender vanilla beans.

Serves 6

Rice pudding:

2/3 cup short-grain rice (preferably arborio)
2 cups milk
1/4 cup sugar
pinch of salt
1 vanilla bean, split lengthwise, seeds scraped out
2 teaspoons butter for greasing
1 egg yolk
1/4 cup heavy cream

Poached cherries:

36 cherries
5 tablespoons butter
1/3 cup sugar
12/3 cups Banyuls
freshly grated nutmeg

To serve (optional):

2 or 3 soft-textured vanilla beans, finely shredded lengthwise

First make the rice pudding. Rinse the rice in cold water, then put into a saucepan, cover with cold water, and bring to a boil. In a large saucepan, heat the milk with the sugar. Drain the rice and add it to the milk, with the salt, and the vanilla bean and seeds. Cook for 10 minutes over a very low heat, then cover with buttered parchment paper so that the rice doesn't dry out, and cook for another 5 minutes.

Mix the egg yolk with the cream. As soon as the rice is cooked, remove from the heat, and stir in the cream mixture. Remove the vanilla bean and cover the rice pudding again with the paper. Set aside at room temperature to allow the flavor to develop until ready to serve.

To prepare the cherries, remove the stalks and pit the fruit, using a cherry pitter.

As you pit them, put the cherries into a bowl of ice water, to encourage them to plump up.

When you are ready to cook the cherries, drain them thoroughly. Heat a frying pan (preferably nonstick). When it is hot, put in the butter and heat until foaming. Quickly sprinkle in half of the sugar and add the cherries. Toss them 2 or 3 times, adding the rest of the sugar as you go, and cook for about 2 minutes.

Pour in two-thirds of the Banyuls. Flambé the cherries and shake the pan. Once the flames have died down, allow the cherries to poach for a minute or two (depending on their ripeness), then transfer them with a slotted spoon to a deep plate.

Pour the remaining Banyuls into the pan and cook to a light syrupy consistency. Spoon this syrup over the cherries and stir in a pinch of nutmeg. For the best flavor, serve the cherries while they are still just warm, arranged around the warm rice pudding. Scatter the shredded vanilla beans, if using, in the middle.

PEELING AND PITTING PEACHES

Make an incision all round the circumference of the peach with the tip of a small knife.

Using a slotted spoon, carefully drop the peach into a saucepan of boiling water (see note).

As soon as the skin splits open at the point of incision, lift out the peach with the slotted spoon, and put it into a bowl of water with ice cubes added.

Take out the peach and peel off the skin, using your fingertips or the tip of the knife; it will come away very easily. If you are not using the peach immediately, rub the flesh lightly with lemon juice to prevent discoloration.

To remove the pit, using a small knife and following the natural line, cut the peach in half through to the pit. Hold the fruit in the palm of your hand and twist the halves in opposite directions so that one half comes away from the pit. Pull out the pit from the other half.

NOTE If the peaches are very ripe, steam them for a few seconds, rather than immerse them in boiling water, to loosen the skins.

poached white peaches with pistachio crème anglaise

I have chosen to poach the peaches in their skins for this recipe, so that the beautiful color of the skin tints the flesh. A judicious hint of rosemary added to the poaching liquid will develop and enhance the flavor of the fruit, but it is essential not to overdo it, or the delicate peach taste will be lost. (Illustrated on page 33.)

Serves 6
6 very ripe white peaches
3/4 cup sugar
a small branch of rosemary
2 cups pistachio crème anglaise (page 32)
6 tiny mint sprigs

Put the peaches in a saucepan large enough to hold them in a single layer. Barely cover them with cold water and add the sugar and rosemary. Bring to a boil over a high heat, then immediately lower the heat, and cook at a low simmer, about 195°F, taking care not to let the liquid boil. Poach the peaches for 5 to 10 minutes, depending on how ripe they are.

When the peaches are cooked, transfer them to a bowl with the poaching syrup and keep at room temperature until ready to serve. Like all poached fruits, they will taste better if they are not refrigerated.

Just before serving, lift the peaches out of the poaching liquid and peel them, with your fingers or a small knife. Halve the fruit and remove the pit.

Put two peach halves in each deep plate, pour a little pistachio crème anglaise around them, lay a sprig of mint on one side, and serve at once.

rhubarb poached in citrus juice topped with coconut flakes

This light, refreshing dessert is so inviting that it will soon disappear...

Serves 4

1 pound rhubarb
juice of 4 oranges
juice of 1 lemon
1 1/4 cups sugar
1 fresh coconut

Peel the rhubarb stalks to remove the fibrous threads, then cut into 2-inch chunks. Rinse in cold water.

Combine the orange juice, lemon juice, and sugar in a saucepan. Bring to a boil over a low heat, stirring occasionally. Put in the rhubarb and poach for 3 to 5 minutes, depending on the thickness of the stalks and the ripeness of the fruit. Whatever you do, don't cook the rhubarb for too long, or it will break down into fibers.

Using a slotted spoon, carefully transfer the rhubarb to a bowl, then reduce the cooking juice by about half. Strain it through a fine conical sieve onto the rhubarb. Allow to cool, then refrigerate for about 1 hour.

To open the coconut, hold it in a cloth in one hand above a bowl (to catch the liquid, which makes a refreshing drink) and, using your other hand, bang it with a hammer or rolling pin.

To serve, divide the rhubarb and juice between serving bowls or small deep plates. Hold the coconut directly above the bowls and scrape the side of a spoon across the flesh, so that curls of different shapes and sizes fall onto the fruit. Serve at once.

poached pears in sauternes

These soft, refreshing winter fruits, with their complex texture and flavor, make the perfect finish to a meal. It is best to serve the pears cold, but absolutely not chilled. Any excess syrup can be churned to make an excellent pear sorbet.

Serves 6

6 to 12 ripe pears, depending on size (preferably Bartlett)
juice and pared zest of 1 orange
1 1/2 cups Sauternes, or other not-too-sweet white wine
3 cups water
2 1/2 tablespoons honey
1 cup sugar
juice of 2 lemons
1 vanilla bean, split
1 cinnamon stick, broken into short lengths
4 cloves

Using a small, sharp knife, score a zigzag pattern in the skin around the top of each pear, working downwards from the stalk. Leaving the zigzag skin at the top in place, peel the rest of each pear very thinly so as to preserve their shape (see photograph). Remove the core from the base, using a corer or small melon baller. Cut the orange zest into thin strips.

Combine all the ingredients in a saucepan big enough to hold everything, including the pears. Set over a medium heat until the liquid comes to a boil, then lower the heat so that it is barely simmering. The cooking time will vary according to the ripeness of the pears. Very ripe pears will only take 5 minutes; much less ripe fruit will need up to 15 minutes. As soon as they are ready, turn off the heat.

Transfer the pears with their poaching syrup to a bowl and set aside at room temperature until needed.

Serve one or two pears on each plate with a little orange zest and some of the syrup.

lightly jellied red fruit consommés

These glorious jellies inspire romance. To enjoy them at their best, use very ripe, flavorful fruit at the height of the season, and serve as a dessert or pre-dessert.

Serves 8

7 ounces strawberries
7 ounces raspberries
7 ounces red currants
7 ounces cherries
3 star anise, or the pared zest of 1 orange, whichever you prefer
1/2 cup sugar
1/2 cup plus 2 tablespoons cold water
4 gelatin leaves, or 1 envelope unflavored gelatin
juice of 1 lemon
red currant sprigs, wild strawberries, lavender sprigs or gooseberries, to decorate

Wash each type of fruit separately, then hull the strawberries and raspberries if necessary. Strip the red currants off their stalks with the prongs of a fork. Pit and halve the cherries. If the strawberries are large, halve them too.

Put all the fruits in a saucepan with the star anise or orange zest, sugar, and ½ cup of the water. Cover the pan tightly with plastic wrap and stand it in a *bain-marie*. Poach over a low heat at 160° to 175°F for about 40 minutes.

Meanwhile, soak the gelatin leaves in cold water to cover, or sprinkle powdered gelatin over 2 table-spoons cold water in a small bowl to soften. Take the saucepan out of the *bain-marie*. Thoroughly drain the gelatin leaves and add them, or the softened powdered gelatin, to the saucepan and gently stir to dissolve the gelatin. Cover with fresh plastic wrap and let cool at room temperature.

Strain the fruit through a cheesecloth-lined sieve or fine conical sieve into a bowl. Add the lemon juice to the liquid. Pour this consommé into small glasses and refrigerate for several hours until lightly set.

Take out of the fridge about 20 minutes before serving and keep at room temperature. Decorate each glass with a sprig of red currants, wild strawberries, sprigs of lavender or a gooseberry.

poached apricots in assam tea syrup

These poached fruits are delicious served on their own in some of their tea-flavored syrup, or with sugar-glazed slices of brioche (illustrated on page 187). You only need to allow three apricots per serving, as they swell slightly during cooking.

Serves 8

24 moist dried apricots
1 1/4 cups sugar
2 cups water
2 tablespoons Assam tea leaves

Put the apricots in a bowl. Combine the sugar and water in a saucepan and dissolve over a medium heat. Bring to the boil, then pour over the fruit and set aside at room temperature for 12 hours.

Pour the syrup into a saucepan; cover the apricots and set aside. Heat the syrup to 160°F (just barely simmering), take the pan off the heat, and add the tea. Cover and leave until almost cold.

Strain the cooled syrup through a fine conical sieve onto the apricots. Leave to infuse for at least 12 hours, to allow the apricots to absorb the aroma of the tea.

grills, roasts, and bakes

Grilling has become increasingly fashionable because it's one of the healthiest cooking methods. I use a ridged griddle pan, which must be preheated until very hot to sear the food on the outside and give an attractive lattice marking, but not overheated or the food will acquire a bitter taste. In the same way, a charcoal grill must be very hot before food is put on the grid. After 5 to 10 minutes cooking, I lower the heat under the griddle pan, or move food to the sides of the grill, so that heat penetrates the center of the food evenly and gently.

Take meat out of the fridge an hour or two before roasting, and preheat the oven to very high for at least 20 minutes, then adjust the setting according to the recipe. Brush the meat with melted butter or oil to help it brown evenly, and baste frequently with the cooking juices or fat to keep the flesh succulent. Halfway through cooking, turn the meat, taking care not to pierce it or the juices will run out. Wrap the cooked meat in foil and let rest for about 10 minutes, so that the flesh relaxes and the juices are retained as you carve it.

As for poultry and game birds, I always remove the wishbone before cooking; this makes carving easier and you can cut the breast into nice even slices. I often bard the birds with thin slices of fatback to make them more tender and succulent.

Small pieces of meat and poultry, and brochettes are delicious grilled, and fill the kitchen with appetizing aromas. Seafood and crustaceans are equally divine; serve these the moment they are cooked.

When grilling, I like to add vine shoots to the charcoal to impart a subtle, succulent flavor. Once the grid has cooled a little, I grill asparagus, slices of eggplant and zucchini, or tomato halves, brushed with olive oil. I serve these drizzled with a trickle of olive oil, a few drops of balsamic vinegar and snipped basil … and enjoy the explosion of flavors in my mouth.

Roasting, which exposes every side of the food to the heat, is more suitable for larger pieces of meat or fish. The traditional Sunday roast, an occasion when the whole family gathers at the table, may be a custom that is fast disappearing, but it's one that we should protect: "the family that eats together stays together."

Always use a roasting pan large enough to allow you to surround the roast with aromatic vegetables like carrots, onions, celery, and garlic; these will flavor the *jus*. Tender roast vegetables (page 124) make a fresh, colorful dish, which I top with a slice of goat cheese.

For baked dishes *en croûte*, like my châteaubriand in a brioche crust (page 138), and sea bream in a fine salt crust (page 134), it is essential to turn the tray during cooking to ensure a superb, evenly golden crust and uniform cooking throughout.

I also use the oven to dry very thin slices of garlic, zucchini, beet, mushrooms, and fennel, or fruits like apple, pineapple, and citrus zest. These are scattered on a baking sheet lined with parchment paper and dried at 145°F to 175°F for an hour or two, depending on thickness and water content. I use a few of these attractive "crisps" to garnish roast meat, poultry or fish, and my *salade gourmande*.

chicken breasts with fennel

This utterly simple dish is full of flavor. For an equally good low fat version, replace the butter and fennel seeds with the candied zest of a lemon.

Serves 4

4 boneless, or partially boned, chicken breasts
2 fennel bulbs
2 large carrots, peeled
2 tablespoons olive oil
2¹/₂ tablespoons butter
1 tablespoon fresh fennel seeds
salt and freshly ground pepper

Marinade:

2 tablespoons runny honey
juice of ¹/₂ lemon
4 tablespoons olive oil
pinch of cayenne pepper

Mix all the marinade ingredients in a wide, shallow bowl, adding a little salt. Add the chicken breasts and turn them to coat thoroughly. Cover with plastic wrap and leave for 1 hour, turning them halfway through.

Cut the fennel lengthwise into ¼-inch slices. Blanch in boiling water for 5 minutes, refresh, and drain. Score the carrots with a zester, cut into ¼-inch diagonal slices, and blanch for 3 minutes; refresh and drain. Lightly brush the fennel and carrots with oil.

Heat a griddle pan until smoking hot. Add the fennel and griddle for 2 minutes, then add the carrots and griddle for another 3 minutes, giving them a quarter-turn to mark a lattice. Turn over and repeat on the other side. Season, place on a plate, and keep hot.

Put the chicken pieces in the hot griddle pan, skin-side down. Once they are marked with lines, quarter-turn to make a lattice pattern. Turn them over, lower the heat, and give them a quarter-turn as before. Cook for 12 to 15 minutes in total, depending on thickness.

Arrange the fennel slices on plates and top with the chicken. Place the carrots alongside. Put a pat of butter on each chicken breast and top with fennel seeds.

medallions of venison with green peppercorn butter

Roe deer venison is a delicate meat that should be treated simply, to preserve all its savors. Fillets of chamois and red deer can be cooked the same way. I serve this with green olive pasta (page 84).

Serves 4

1 tenderloin of venison (preferably roe deer),
1¹/₂ to 1³/₄ pounds
salt and freshly ground pepper
watercress leaves, to garnish

Marinade:

6 tablespoons olive oil
few thyme sprigs
2 bay leaves, quartered
2 garlic cloves, peeled and thinly sliced
10 black peppercorns, crushed
5 juniper berries, crushed

Green peppercorn butter:

7 tablespoons butter, softened
juice of 1 lemon
16 green peppercorns in brine, rinsed and crushed

Cut the venison tenderloin into 8 medallions. Mix together all the marinade ingredients. Put the medallions into a deep dish, cover with the marinade (for method, see quick meat marinade, page 14), and allow to marinate for 1 hour.

Meanwhile, mix together the ingredients for the green peppercorn butter and season with a little salt.

Heat a griddle pan until very hot. Season the medallions very lightly, put them on the griddle, and cook for 1 minute, then give them a quarter-turn to obtain a lattice marking. Cook for another minute, then turn them over and repeat. The precise timing will depend on how well done you like your meat.

To serve, place 2 medallions on each plate and top with a generous amount of the flavored butter. Garnish with a few watercress leaves on the side.

grilled fillet of lamb with mediterranean vegetables

This is one of the recipes I love to cook when I stay at my house in the south of France. The confit vegetables add an unusual modern twist, and the dish brings together many of the typical products of the region.

You will need to bone a whole saddle of lamb (or get your butcher to do this for you); keep the bones to make the *jus*. Much of the dish can be prepared in advance, as you can cook the vegetables beforehand and keep them covered. Just reheat them and the *jus* a few minutes before you assemble the dish. Only the meat needs to be cooked at the last moment.

Serves 4

2 lamb fillets from a saddle, trimmed of all fat and membrane, each about $1/2$ pound (bones reserved)
1 onion, peeled and cut into small pieces
1 carrot, peeled and coarsely chopped
6 tablespoons dry white wine
6 savory sprigs
1 small bouquet garni
$7/8$ cup water
1 zucchini, about 7 ounces
2 eggplants, preferably long thin ones, about $3/4$ pound in total
5 tablespoons olive oil
10 ounces confit tomatoes (page 79, about $1/2$ recipe)
4 unpeeled confit garlic cloves (page 80), optional
8 black olives, pitted and cut into small strips
salt and freshly ground pepper

First make the *jus*. Preheat the oven to 425°F. Put the lamb bones in a roasting pan and place in the hot oven to color for 15 minutes. Add the onion and carrot, cook until browned, then deglaze the roasting pan with the white wine and simmer until reduced by half. Transfer everything to a saucepan and add 2 savory sprigs, the bouquet garni, and water. Cook gently until reduced by half, then strain through a cheesecloth-lined sieve. Pour the *jus* back into the saucepan, return to the heat, and reduce to a slightly syrupy consistency. Season with salt and pepper and keep at room temperature.

To grill the vegetables, heat a ridged griddle pan. Using a mandoline slicer or sharp knife, cut the zucchini and eggplant into long slices, about $1/8$ inch thick. Lay these flat on the work surface, season with salt, and brush with a smear of olive oil. Place in the griddle pan and grill for 30 seconds to 1 minute, depending on the heat of the pan, until marked with brown lines. Give the vegetables a quarter-turn to make a criss-cross pattern, then turn them over and repeat on the other side. Put all the grilled vegetables on a plate and keep them warm.

To cook the lamb fillets, smear both sides and the cut ends with a touch of olive oil and grill in the same way as the vegetables, until they are marked with an attractive lattice pattern on both sides and feel springy when pressed; they will now be cooked pink. If you prefer lamb cooked further, roast them in a hot oven for 5 minutes for medium, or 10 minutes for well done. Wrap the fillets loosely in foil and let rest for 5 minutes before carving.

To assemble the dish, unwrap the lamb, season with salt, and carve into thin slices. Lay a slice of eggplant on each plate. Place a few warm confit tomatoes on top, cover with a zucchini slice, add a few more tomatoes, then another eggplant slice. Finally add half a sliced lamb fillet to each serving. Top with a confit garlic clove if using. Pour the warm *jus* over the meat and vegetables, scatter on a few olive strips, lay a sprig of savory in the *jus* on one side of each plate, and serve right away.

fish brochettes

Spices give these unusual brochettes a special flavor – mustard intensifies the taste of the monkfish, while cumin seeds give the salmon a sweet spiciness. Lime leaves protect the scallops from the heat and impart a subtle flavor. The potatoes hold the fish in place, and taste good too. You will need 8-inch skewers; if wooden, presoak in warm water to prevent burning. Salad leaves are the ideal accompaniment; or you might like to serve a hollandaise sauce (page 20) spiked with a spoonful of fresh tomato coulis.

Serves 4

1/2 pound middle-cut salmon fillet, skinned
6 ounces monkfish fillet, from the middle or head end
1 teaspoon cumin seeds
1 tablespoon English mustard powder
4 shelled plump sea scallops, each about 2 ounces
4 fresh lime or lemon leaves, blanched (optional)
2 tablespoons olive oil
4 small new potatoes, parboiled and halved widthwise
salt

To serve:

arugula, purslane, or corn salad (mâche)
fennel fronds (optional)
lemon wedges

Cut both the salmon and monkfish fillet into 4 cubes. Roll the salmon in cumin seeds. Carefully dry the monkfish cubes, then roll in the mustard powder. Lightly salt the scallops. Smear the lime leaves with olive oil, then roll one around each scallop.

Thread a potato half onto each skewer, with the rounded side facing outwards. Add a monkfish cube, then a wrapped scallop, a piece of salmon, and finally another potato half.

Preheat the broiler or griddle pan until very hot. Drizzle a trickle of olive oil over the brochettes, salt them lightly and broil or grill for 4 to 5 minutes, turning every minute; the fish will be lightly cooked. If you prefer, cook it for another 2 to 3 minutes.

Place a brochette on each plate and arrange a few salad leaves to one side, scattering with some fennel fronds, if you like. Serve with lemon wedges.

grilled lobster with garden herbs

A garnish of asparagus tips will set off this simple, delicate dish to perfection. For an extra treat, serve with a hollandaise sauce (page 20).

Serves 4

4 live lobsters, just under 1 pound each
8 tablespoons olive oil
juice of 1 lemon
few rosemary sprigs, 2 thyme sprigs, 1 dill sprig, and 2 tarragon sprigs
small bunch of flat-leaf parsley
salt and freshly ground pepper
small bunch of watercress, to garnish
1 lemon, cut into wedges, to serve

Put the lobsters in a plastic bag in the freezer for 2 hours, then remove from the bag and plunge into a large pan of boiling water for 30 seconds. Drain and split them in half lengthwise with a large knife, starting at the head and pressing down firmly, then repeating at the tail end. Remove the gritty sac from the head, the intestines and black intestinal thread. Reserve the coral, if any, to use in a sauce.

For the marinade, mix 4 tablespoons olive oil with the lemon juice in a dish and put in the lobster halves, flesh-side down. Let marinate for 20 minutes.

Meanwhile, chop all the herbs very finely and mix with the remaining 4 tablespoons olive oil.

To cook, preheat a griddle pan. When it's very hot, season the lobsters with salt and place, flesh-side down, on the griddle. Cook for 2 minutes, giving them a quarter-turn to obtain a lattice marking, then turn over and cook for another 2 to 3 minutes; to check that they are tender, pierce with the tip of a knife.

Place 2 lobster halves on each plate, flesh-side up. Season with pepper and drizzle with a few drops of herb oil. Garnish with watercress and serve with lemon.

quail brochettes with almond-stuffed dates

The world has been my inspiration for these extraordinary brochettes – China for the spice and mushrooms, the Middle East for dates and nuts, and Italy for the mozzarella.

They are ideal for a summer cookout. In winter, you can cook them in a griddle pan. When fresh almonds are out of season, use dried ones and soak them in cold water for at least 24 hours.

For an extra touch of exoticism, I serve the brochettes on a bed of dark rice, using two-thirds wild rice and one-third black rice. The black rice gives a softer texture to the wild rice, which is rather too spiky on its own.

Serves 4

4 plump quails
8 fresh dates
8 skinned almonds, preferably fresh (or blanched)

Marinade:

1 tablespoon honey
1 tablespoon lemon juice
1/2 teaspoon five-spice powder

Skewers:

2 large onions, preferably red
handful of coarse salt
8 dried Chinese wood ear mushrooms, soaked in
cold water for 6 hours
1 red bell pepper, halved, cored, and seeded
8 mini mozzarella balls
2 tablespoons olive oil
salt and freshly ground pepper

Preheat the oven to 400°F. Put the marinade ingredients in a small saucepan, stand it in a *bain-marie* and bring to a boil, stirring occasionally, then set aside to cool.

Part-roast the onions in their skins on a bed of coarse salt for 20 minutes and let cool. Drain the soaked dried mushrooms and cook in lightly salted water for 20 minutes, then drain and set aside.

Meanwhile, pit the dates and insert an almond into the cavity.

To prepare the stuffed quail, remove the wishbone, using the point of a small knife.

Using a boning knife, carefully cut the meat from the breastbone, following the contours of the bones, and making sure the 2 breast halves are held together as one piece. (Keep the legs to use in another dish, or grill them and serve to accompany the brochettes.)

Lay the butterflied quail breasts skin-side down and make an incision in the thickest part of each half.

Insert a date in each incision in the quail breasts. Add the stuffed quail breasts to the cold marinade and leave for about 30 minutes, turning them over after 15 minutes.

Close the butterflied quail breasts, and secure the opening with toothpicks.

It is best to use metal skewers for the brochettes. Cut the red pepper into eight 1-inch squares. Skin and quarter the part-roasted onions, then thread a quarter onto each skewer. Wrap each mini mozzarella in a Chinese mushroom and thread one onto each skewer, followed by a red pepper square. Carefully thread a stuffed whole quail breast onto each skewer. Next, thread on a square of pepper, another mushroom-wrapped mozzarella ball and finally another onion quarter. Brush the brochettes with a touch of olive oil and season them lightly.

If possible, cook the brochettes on a grill, or use a hot griddle pan. Turn them every 2 minutes, allowing 8 minutes if you like your quail cooked pink, or 10 minutes if you prefer them medium. Slide the contents of the skewers delicately onto a bed of boiled dark rice. If you like, cut the quail breasts in half to reveal the almond-stuffed dates.

grilled confit of rabbit and apples with walnuts

This dish takes very little time to put together. The fruity flavor of the grilled apples marries very well with the rabbit, while the radicchio and mâche salad adds a refreshing note. (Illustrated on page 81.)

Serves 4

4 confit rabbit legs (page 80)
4 confit rabbit shoulders (page 80)
2 small, fairly tart apples
3 tablespoons walnut oil
1 tablespoon cider vinegar
7 ounces radicchio or treviso, separated into leaves and washed
3 1/2 ounces corn salad (mâche), washed
8 walnuts, preferably "wet" (fresh), peeled, halved, and soaked in a little milk
salt and freshly ground pepper

Set a large griddle pan over a high heat. Put in the rabbit legs and cook for 2 to 3 minutes, then give them a quarter-turn to make an attractive criss-cross pattern. After another 2 to 3 minutes, turn them over and repeat on the other side. Lower the heat and move the rabbit legs to the edge of the griddle, where it is less hot. Put the shoulders in the middle of the pan and cook in the same way as the legs. After 8 to 12 minutes, all 8 pieces will be ready. Remove them from the griddle and keep warm.

Cut the apples horizontally into rings, about ¼ inch thick. Place them on the very hot griddle and grill for about 1 minute on each side, giving them a quarter-turn halfway through.

To assemble the dish, make a vinaigrette with the walnut oil, cider vinegar, and a little salt and pepper. Use it to dress the radicchio and corn salad. Arrange a bouquet of salad on 4 serving plates and prop a rabbit leg and shoulder against the salad. Put 2 apple rings on one side of each plate. Drain the walnut halves and divide them between the plates.

tender roast vegetables with goat cheese

This refreshing starter, with its myriad of colors, flavors, and textures, is a feast for the eye as well as the palate. Depending on the season and what's in the market, you can substitute any delicate vegetables, as long as they are tender.

Serves 4

12 small, young artichokes (the kind you can eat whole), optional
3 tablespoons dry white wine
1 cup olive oil
juice of 1/2 lemon
1 red and 1 green bell pepper
1 small eggplant
4 baby zucchini
1 small fennel bulb, peeled
8 ears baby corn
12 asparagus tips
4 unpeeled garlic cloves
2 medium red onions, peeled and cut into wedges
2 thyme sprigs
2 bay leaves
18 seedless red grapes, peeled and halved
2 tablespoons sugar
12 cherry tomatoes
1/4 cup pumpkin seeds
4 slices of creamy goat cheese, cut from a log
salt and freshly ground pepper

If you are including artichokes, cut off the tips of the leaves, using a sharp knife, and pare the base to leave only the tender part of the stalk and the heart. Put the artichokes in a small saucepan with the white wine, 1 tablespoon olive oil, and the lemon juice. Add enough water to cover and cook gently for 4 minutes, until half-cooked and still slightly crunchy. Leave the artichokes in their cooking liquid at room temperature until cold, then drain them.

Preheat the oven to 400°F. Peel the peppers with a swivel peeler, halve them lengthwise, remove the seeds and white membranes, and cut the peppers into thin strips. Cut the eggplant and zucchini into rounds, about 1/2 inch thick.

Parboil the fennel in boiling water for 8 minutes, refresh, drain, and cut into 8 wedges. Cut each ear of corn into 3 pieces, blanch in boiling water for 3 minutes, refresh, and drain. Blanch the asparagus for 2 minutes, then refresh and drain.

Heat 3 tablespoons olive oil in a small roasting pan, add the garlic and onion segments, and brown them lightly for 2 to 3 minutes. Add the thyme and bay leaves and place in the oven.

Heat 2 tablespoons olive oil in a frying pan. Season the eggplant rounds with salt and pepper and fry over a medium heat on both sides until golden. Remove and set aside at room temperature.

Heat another 3 tablespoons oil in the pan. Add the pepper strips, sweat and color them for 5 minutes, then add them to the onions (in the oven).

Add another 6 tablespoons olive oil to the frying pan, put in the zucchini, fennel, and artichokes, and fry over a medium heat for 3 minutes. Add the baby corn and fry for another 2 minutes. Transfer the contents of the frying pan to the roasting pan and return it to the oven.

In a small frying pan, sauté the grapes with the sugar over a high heat until lightly caramelized, then add them, the eggplant, and the asparagus, to the other vegetables in the roasting pan.

Heat the remaining olive oil in the same frying pan, add the tomatoes and cook over a medium heat until golden. As soon as they are colored, put them with all the other vegetables. Using a slotted spoon, delicately stir all the vegetables together and season to taste. Roast in the oven for another 5 minutes.

Lightly salt the pumpkin seeds, sprinkle with a few drops of olive oil, and toast lightly under a low grill. Divide the vegetables between 4 plates, piling them into a dome. Remove the thyme and bay leaves. Scatter over the toasted pumpkin seeds, top with a slice of goat cheese, and serve piping hot.

roast leg of lamb with garlic and fresh anchovies

Before roasting a leg of lamb, I like to remove the bone and stud the meat with garlic and fresh anchovy fillets, a combination that imparts a superb flavor. The roasting time will, of course, be determined by the weight, and whether you like your lamb rare, medium, or well done.

Lamb on the bone can be roasted in the same way, though it takes less time to cook because the bone conducts the heat through the meat. Simply omit the anchovies, stud the surface with the halved garlic cloves, and allow 10 minutes per pound after the initial roasting.

Serves 8

1 leg of lamb, about 5^1/$_2$ pounds
8 fresh anchovy fillets, frozen until firm
3 to 4 garlic cloves, peeled and halved
3 tablespoons softened butter, or clarified butter (page 188)
2 carrots, peeled and coarsely chopped
2 medium onions, peeled and quartered
1 head of garlic (unpeeled), halved widthwise
2 bay leaves
few thyme or rosemary sprigs
salt and freshly ground pepper

Jus:

^{7}/$_8$ cup red or white wine, according to taste
1^1/$_4$ cups water

Preheat the oven to 425°F. To bone the lamb, tunnel into the meat using a boning knife and, working from the ball end, cut around the exposed bone, gradually working deeper and cutting through the tendons to free the leg bone. Cut out the cartilage, then remove the bone from the other end. Set aside the bones and trimmings.

Make 6 to 8 incisions in the lamb with the tip of a pointed knife, spacing them well apart. Insert a frozen anchovy fillet in each cut and push it right into

To check if the lamb is cooked, insert an instant meat thermometer into the thickest part of the meat for 15 seconds; it should read 125°F for pink meat, or 135°F to 140°F for medium to well done. Or insert a fine skewer for 10 seconds, take it out, and press it against your wrist; if it feels warm, the lamb is cooked. The juices that run from where you pierced the meat should be almost clear and transparent.

Take the lamb out of the roasting pan and wrap it loosely in foil; leaving a gap for air to enter will prevent further cooking and stop the meat from steaming. Let rest for 15 to 20 minutes before carving; this allows the meat to relax and helps to keep in the juices, making the meat beautifully tender. Meanwhile, make the *jus* (see below).

Once the meat has rested, carve it into even slices. Arrange on plates and spoon over some of the jus. Serve accompanied by vegetables of your choice, with the remaining *jus* handed separately in a sauce boat.

Jus

To make the *jus*, tip the pan and ladle out most of the fat that runs into the corner.

Set the roasting pan over a medium heat. Pour in the wine to deglaze the pan, lightly scraping the base of the pan to dissolve the sediment that has stuck to it.

Cook until the wine has reduced by half, then add 1¼ cups water. Reduce the liquid again by half. Strain it though a fine sieve or cheesecloth to obtain a light gravy or *jus*. Season to taste with salt and pepper. It is important to add the pepper at the end of cooking to ensure all of its pungency is retained.

the meat, using the knife tip. Do the same with the 3 to 4 halved, peeled garlic cloves, making a small incision for each and pushing them in.

Tie up the lamb with string, securing it in about a dozen places to make a neat roast. Rub the surface with softened or clarified butter and season with salt. Put the lamb in a medium roasting pan. Scatter the carrots, onions, halved garlic bulb, and herbs around the meat, then finally, add the bones and trimmings.

Roast in the oven for 50 minutes initially. Baste the lamb with the cooking juices and return it to the oven. Roast for another 12 minutes per pound for pink lamb, basting the meat every 15 minutes or so, and turning it over on to the other side halfway through to ensure even cooking and prevent the meat from drying out. (If you prefer your lamb cooked for longer, allow 16 minutes per pound for medium, or 22 minutes per pound for well done lamb.)

roast stuffed festive goose

This superb Christmas or New Year dish makes a change from the traditional turkey, which appears too often for my taste on such occasions. Little steamed stuffed cabbages (page 99) are the perfect accompaniment. Any leftover goose and stuffing makes a delicious cold feast, served with my pickled plums (page 188).

Don't try to use a food processor to make the stuffing; if you do not have a meat grinder, ask the butcher to grind the pork and fat for you.

Serves 8

1 goose, about 9 pounds, with a little of the neck skin attached
1/2 pound onions, peeled and cut into large pieces
1/2 pound carrots, peeled and cut into large pieces
small bunch of thyme
2 bay leaves
1 cup dry white wine
1 cup water
salt and freshly ground pepper

Stuffing:

1 1/2 pounds pork fatback
3/4 pound bacon
1 1/4 cups chopped curly parsley
2/3 cup chopped onion
3 tablespoons butter
1/2 pound button mushrooms, chopped
2 to 3 teaspoons salt
3/4 teaspoon freshly milled pepper
4 slices crustless white bread, diced and soaked in 3/4 cup milk
2 eggs
7/8 cup heavy cream, well chilled
3 tablespoons Cognac (optional)

First make the stuffing. Put the pork and bacon through a meat grinder, using the medium blade. Place in a bowl with the parsley. Lightly sweat the onion in the butter until softened, then add the mushrooms, and cook until

tender. Add to the meat with the seasoning. Stand the bowl over another bowl of crushed ice and beat the mixture with a wooden spoon for 3 to 4 minutes, until well mixed. Lightly squeeze the bread to remove excess milk, then add to the mixture, with the eggs. Mix for 2 minutes, then add the cream, and Cognac if using, and stir the mixture for another 3 to 4 minutes. Cover with plastic wrap and refrigerate until needed.

Preheat the oven to 350°F. Lift up the skin covering the front of the goose breast and take out the wishbone with a small knife. Turn the goose over onto the breast, and season the body cavity with a generous pinch of salt. Stretch out the neck skin as far as it will go, and put on as much stuffing as you can, pushing it as far towards the start of the breast as possible. Fold the skin back over the stuffing and, using a trussing needle threaded with kitchen string, sew up the skin to make a sort of jabot, so that the stuffing cannot escape during cooking. Put the goose into a roasting pan (without added fat, as it's a fatty bird). Place any remaining stuffing on a lightly buttered sheet of foil, and roll up into a fat sausage shape.

Roast the goose in the hot oven for 30 minutes. Baste with the fat that is rendered, then pour off most of it, and add the onions, carrots, thyme, and bay leaves to the pan. Roast for another 1 1/4 hours, basting every 20 minutes. Put the stuffing "sausage" (if you have made one) into the roasting pan alongside the goose after the first 20 minutes.

Transfer the cooked goose to a serving platter, cover loosely with foil so that the skin remains crisp and let rest in a warm place. Leave the stuffing in its foil roll, and set aside with the goose.

To make the *jus*, pour off the fat from the roasting pan. Set the pan over a high heat and deglaze with the wine. Reduce by half, then add 1 cup water, reduce by half again, and strain through a conical sieve. Season to taste, and keep warm. To serve, using scissor tips, carefully cut the string that is holding the stuffing in the neck skin, and discard it. Unwrap the stuffing "sausage" and cut it into slices.

Carve thin slices of breast meat. Cut off the legs from the carcass, serving only the thigh meat cut into long slices. Serve the goose with a little stuffing from the neck or "sausage," and the *jus*.

roast duckling with cloves, honey, and spices

This springtime dish is very popular at The Waterside Inn. My manager, Diego Masciaga, carves it in the dining room with magical dexterity, into elegant thin slices, to the admiration of all my guests. Don't forget to warn your guests to pick out the cloves with their forks and discard them, as they have a very aggressive taste.

The perfect garnish for these ducklings with their oriental overtone would be bok choy tempura. Add an extra 2 teaspoons cornstarch to the tempura batter (page 152), to make the deep-fried bok choy leaves extra crunchy.

Serves 4

2 ducklings (preferably Long Island or Challandais), each about 3 pounds, wishbones removed, trussed

20 cloves

5 tablespoons runny honey

juice of 1/2 lemon

1 tablespoon olive oil

generous pinch of pain d'épices spices (ground mixed ginger, cloves, cinnamon, and star anise)

1 large onion, peeled and cut into medium dice

2 large carrots, peeled and cut into medium dice

2 thyme sprigs

1 1/4 cups chicken stock (page 16), or water

salt and freshly ground pepper

Preheat the oven to 400°F. Bring a large saucepan of lightly salted water to a boil. Put in the ducklings and blanch them for 3 minutes. Transfer to a bowl of ice water and leave for 5 minutes, then drain well and pat dry.

Stick the cloves into the duckling breasts, spacing them evenly and well apart.

Mix the honey with the lemon juice, olive oil, and ground spices. Put the ducklings in a roasting pan, brush generously with the honey and spice mixture, and immediately place in the hot oven. Roast for 5 minutes.

Baste the duckling with the liquid bubbling in the pan. Spread the onions, carrots, and thyme around the ducklings, and continue to roast for another 20 minutes for pink duck, basting after 10 minutes. If you prefer your duck cooked medium to well done, roast for another 10 minutes.

When the ducklings are cooked, cut off the legs, wrap the rest of the birds loosely in foil and keep them warm. Grill or broil the legs for about 10 minutes, preferably in a griddle pan, giving them a quarter-turn after 2 to 3 minutes to give an attractive lattice marking, then turning them over to repeat on the other side.

To make the sauce, deglaze the roasting pan containing the honey-caramelized vegetables with the stock or water. Set over a medium heat, reduce the liquid by two-thirds to make a slightly syrupy sauce, then strain it through a conical sieve. Season with salt and pepper and keep warm.

To serve, carve off the duck breasts. Cut each twice on the diagonal, first in one direction, then in the other, to obtain 6 good chunky pieces from each breast. Arrange 6 pieces pell-mell on each plate, and place a leg on one side. Spoon off any fat from the sauce, then drizzle a few drops of sauce around the plates. Serve the rest separately in a sauce boat.

roast-poached stuffed loin of pork

This double cooking method of roasting and poaching makes the meat appetizingly golden on the outside, yet wonderfully succulent on the inside, and produces a rich, yet delicate gravy. I like to serve the pork with braised Belgian endive and steamed or boiled snow peas; the contrasting melting and crisp textures are perfectly balanced.

Serves 4

1¹/₂ pounds boned pork loin (about 2¹/₄ pounds on the bone)
7 ounces pig's caul, or 2 very thin strips of pork fat
4 tablespoons clarified butter (see page 188)
2 carrots, peeled and chopped
1 onion, peeled and chopped
1¹/₂ quarts chicken stock (page 16)
1 bouquet garni
salt and freshly ground pepper

Stuffing:

1 tablespoon butter
²/₃ ounce salt pork (or 2 slices bacon), finely diced
3 tablespoons finely diced celery
3 tablespoons finely chopped onion
¹/₂ small apple, peeled, cored, and chopped
2 medium plums (preferably Victoria or quetsche), pitted and finely diced
pinch of sugar
2 tablespoons coarse dry white bread crumbs
2 tablespoons chopped parsley

First make the stuffing. Heat the butter in a saucepan, add the diced pork or bacon, and cook until golden brown. Transfer to a bowl with a slotted spoon and set aside.

Add the celery and onion to the pork fat in the pan and sweat gently for 2 minutes. Add the apple, plums, and sugar, and cook over a medium heat for about 20 minutes, stirring with a wooden spatula from time to time.

Now add the bread crumbs, parsley, and fried pork, mix well and cook over a low heat for 5 minutes, stirring continuously. Season the stuffing to taste with salt and pepper. Transfer to a bowl and let cool, then cover and refrigerate for at least 2 hours.

To prepare the pork loin, use a carving knife with a very long, thin, pointed blade to make an incision all the way through the middle of the meat. Using a circular sawing movement, cut out a small hole. Pull out the knife blade, making sure that all the meat from inside the hole comes out with it, leaving a cavity for the stuffing.

Insert a funnel with a fairly wide nozzle into one end of the cavity. Put in half the stuffing and push it in with your thumb. Repeat from the other end. Wrap the caul or pork fat around the pork loin to prevent the stuffing escaping from either end, and tie it in place with a few knots of kitchen string.

The first cooking stage is roasting the pork. Preheat the oven to 425°F. Melt the clarified butter in a roasting pan. Put in the stuffed pork, season with salt and pepper, and cook for about 6 minutes, until colored all over. Add the carrots and onion and roast in the hot oven for 35 minutes, basting with the cooking juices every 10 minutes.

Now it is time to poach the pork. Pour the chicken stock into a long, shallow pan and bring to a boil. Put in the pork, carrots, and onion, taking care not to include any of the cooking fat. Add the bouquet garni and poach at 160°F for 50 minutes, skimming off any scum from the surface whenever necessary. Lift out the pork and remove the string and caul or fat. Wrap the pork loin in foil and keep it warm.

Reduce the cooking liquor over a high heat until it very lightly coats the back of a spoon. Discard the bouquet garni. Season the gravy with salt and pepper to taste, then strain through a conical sieve into a jug or bowl; keep hot.

To serve, carve 3 or 4 neat slices per serving. Arrange on plates, with the accompanying vegetables. Spoon the gravy over the pork, taking care to avoid drizzling any over the stuffing.

sea bream in a fine salt crust

My son Alain created this recipe, which he often cooks at The Waterside Inn. It reflects his talent for artistic simplicity, which I admire. Baking the sea bream in a salt crust highlights both the visual impact of the marbled flesh and the flavor. Other whole fish, such as sea bass, can be cooked in the same way.

Serves 2

1 sea bream, about 1³/4 pounds, gutted through the belly, gills removed, scaled, and trimmed
3 thyme or fennel sprigs
3 herb crêpes (page 58), 11 or 12 inches in diameter

Salt crust:

2 egg whites
1 pound fine salt

Garnish:

3¹/2 tablespoons chive oil (page 188), optional
2 lemon wedges

Lay the fish on a double thickness of foil and put the thyme or fennel sprigs inside the belly. Trim the foil with scissors, following the contours of the fish and leaving a ¾-inch border all around; set aside.

Lay 2 crêpes on the work surface, overlapping them slightly, and place the sea bream on top (see above). Fold the crêpes over the fish to enclose it.

Use the third crêpe to cover the exposed parts, trimming it with scissors if necessary. The fish should be completely covered, but the crêpes must only overlap very slightly.

Preheat the oven to 400°F. Sprinkle a little fine salt onto the center of a baking sheet (this helps the fish

to cook evenly). Lay the foil on the salt, then place the fish on the foil.

For the salt crust, beat the egg whites until half-risen, then add the salt and continue to beat until the whites are firm and smooth, like a meringue. Using a palette knife, spread evenly over the entire surface of the bream, taking it right down to the foil to make an airtight seal. Smooth the surface, then using the end of a small palette knife, trace the head, mouth and eye of the fish. Press down very lightly with the end of the palette knife to imitate scales (see below right) and finally trace the tail.

Very carefully transfer the baking sheet to the oven, taking care not to jolt it, which might cause the foil holding the fish to slip on the salt.

Bake for 20 minutes, then insert a trussing needle or fine knife tip into the thickest part of the fish for 10 seconds to check if it is cooked; the needle should feel just hot when you withdraw it. If it is lukewarm, the fish needs a little longer.

Serve the bream without delay, presenting it in its salt crust. You can either leave it on the baking sheet, or slide it on the foil onto an oval platter lined with a napkin. At the table or in the kitchen, use a knife tip to cut open the crust, following the traced line of the head, then along the length of the body. Lift off the salt crust to release an instant waft of sea-scented steam, then carefully lift off the crêpes, and peel away the skin with the knife blade to reveal the natural perfection of the fish.

Lift off the fillets with a knife and arrange them on 2 plates. If you wish, drizzle with chive oil, and garnish with lemon wedges. (Illustrated on page 6.)

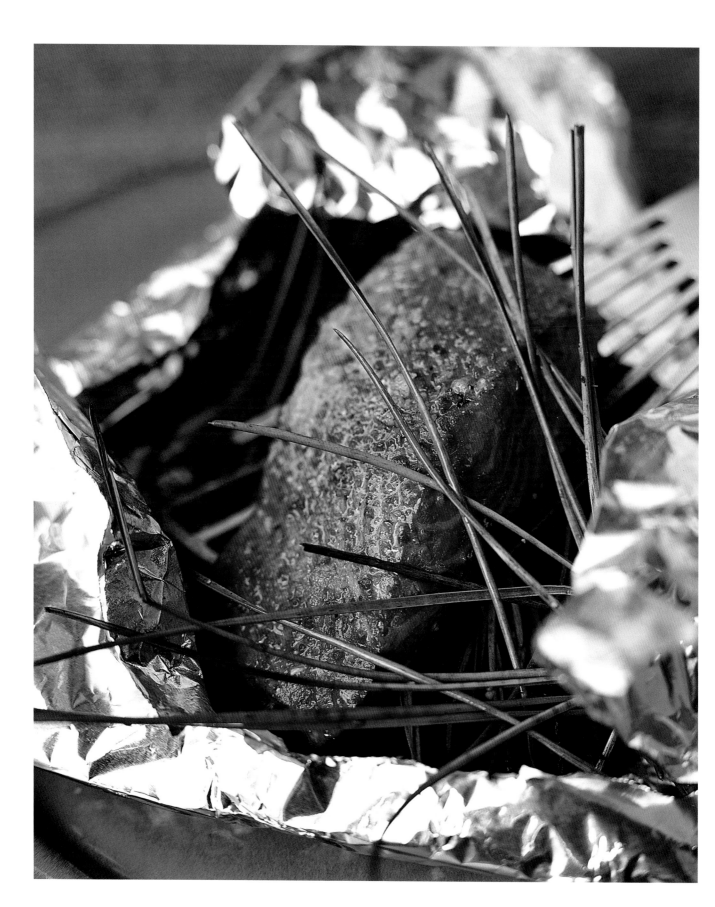

salmon en papillote with pine needles

I adore this dish, which Alain put together. As the salmon cooks, the sea-scented pine needles infuse it with their flavor in an extraordinary way. The technique is simple, but the concept is brilliant. Serve with lemon wedges, and lettuce dressed with olive oil vinaigrette; or a light *nage* with star anise and a few pieces of sea lettuce added.

Serves 4

4 pieces of unskinned salmon fillet cut from the back, each about 1/2 pound
1 tablespoon white peppercorns, crushed
1 1/2 teaspoons coriander seeds, crushed
2 tablespoons sea salt flakes
6 tablespoons olive oil
1/4 pound long, marine pine needles, lightly rinsed in water, if necessary, and dried

Preheat the oven to 350°F. Make two light incisions in the skin of each salmon fillet with a knife. Mix the crushed pepper, coriander seeds, and salt flakes. Smear both sides of the fillets with olive oil and sprinkle the flesh side with the seasoning mixture. Roll the pine needles in the remaining olive oil.

Cut a double thickness of foil into four 10-inch squares. Divide the pine needles into 4 portions. Put two-thirds of each portion in the center of each foil square. Place a salmon fillet on top, skin-side down, and sprinkle with the remaining pine needles.

Loosely fold up the ends of the foil to meet in the middle, fold them over, and pinch the edges together to seal, without wrapping the fish too tightly.

Place the papillotes on a baking tray. Put this on a heat diffuser or direct heat for 5 minutes, then transfer to the oven and cook for 5 minutes if you like your salmon pink in the middle. Give it another 5 minutes in the oven if you prefer it well done.

To serve, slide the papillotes onto serving plates, open them up to reveal the contents, and present to your guests so they can appreciate the aroma. Remove the pine needles before the salmon is eaten.

minted carrot and pumpkin pastilla

New season's carrots and pumpkin infuse this flaky hors d'oeuvre with sweet, spicy nuances, while a squeeze of orange juice adds freshness.

Serves 6

1 1/2 pounds pumpkin, peeled and cubed
6 tablespoons olive oil
2/3 cup thinly sliced new or baby onions
1 1/4 pounds new carrots, cut into thin rounds
5 tablespoons pine nuts, lightly toasted
1/3 cup golden raisins, blanched in sugar syrup (page 188)
1 teaspoon grated fresh ginger
large pinch of ground cinnamon
2 tablespoons snipped mint
12 sheets of phyllo pastry, cut in 8-inch rounds
salt and freshly ground pepper
confectioners' sugar, to dust
1 orange, cut into 6 wedges, to serve

Preheat the oven to 350°F. Steam the pumpkin cubes until almost disintegrating, place in a bowl and crush with a fork. Heat a little oil in a saucepan, add the onions and sweat over low heat for 2 minutes. Add the carrots and cook gently to soften; they should retain a slight crunch. Add to the pumpkin with the pine nuts, raisins, ginger, and cinnamon. Mix well, season and stir in the mint. Cool completely.

Oil a deep ovenproof earthenware or cast-iron dish, 6 inches in diameter. Lay a sheet of phyllo in the dish, brush with oil, then place another phyllo sheet on top and brush with oil. Spread a thin layer of the vegetable mixture on top. Continue to layer in this way to use all the filling and phyllo, finishing with two layers of oiled phyllo. Bake in the oven for 15 to 20 minutes.

Dust the cooked pastilla with confectioners' sugar, and briefly place under a hot broiler until the sugar is slightly melted (don't let it burn). Slide the pastilla out of the baking dish onto a serving plate, or serve it from the dish. It will crumble as you cut it, but this won't spoil the appearance. Serve with orange wedges.

châteaubriand in a brioche crust

The difference between this recipe and a classic châteaubriand en croûte is the brioche crust, which is crisp and golden on the outside, yet meltingly soft inside. I serve it with a hollandaise sauce (page 20) enhanced with a generous handful of snipped chervil. The combination of mushrooms, beef, and sauce is exceptionally good. When fresh cèpes are in season, I use them instead of button mushrooms.

Normally a châteaubriand is a beef tenderloin cut to serve two, but this dish is better suited to serving four. It can be assembled up to 3 hours before the final cooking – ideal for entertaining.

Serves 4

1³/4 to 2 pounds trimmed tenderloin of beef, cut from the top end to the middle
¹/4 cup clarified butter (page 188)
12 good spinach leaves

Mushroom duxelle:

3 tablespoons butter
14 ounces button mushrooms, wiped and finely chopped
juice of 1 lemon
¹/2 cup finely chopped shallots
4 tablespoons heavy cream

To assemble:

14 ounces brioche dough (page 186, about ¹/2 recipe)
flour for dusting
3 herb crêpes (page 58), 11 to 12 inches in diameter
1 egg yolk beaten with 1 teaspoon milk (egg wash)
salt and freshly ground pepper

First make the mushroom duxelle. Heat the butter in a frying pan over a medium heat. Add the mushrooms and lemon juice and cook for a few minutes, until all the liquid has evaporated. Add the shallots and cook

until softened, then add the cream and cook, stirring continuously, until it is all absorbed. Season to taste, transfer to a bowl, and let cool, then refrigerate.

To pre-cook the beef, preheat the oven to 400°F. Heat the clarified butter in a roasting pan. Season the beef with salt and pepper, put it in the roasting pan, and sear over a medium heat for 3 to 5 minutes, until golden brown all over. Put the pan in the oven and roast the beef for 7 minutes, turning it over halfway through. At this stage, the beef will be very rare. Take it out of the oven, place on a rack and let cool.

Briefly blanch the spinach leaves, refresh them, and spread out to drain on a dish towel.

To assemble, roll out the brioche dough on a lightly floured surface to a rectangle, roughly 10 x 14 inches and ¹/8 inch thick. Lay 2 crêpes slightly overlapping along the middle, letting them overhang the ends by about 2 inches. Cover with a few spinach leaves. Using a spoon, spread a ¹/2-inch band of mushroom duxelle down the middle of the crêpes. Put the cold fillet of beef on top and cover the whole surface, including the ends, with the remaining duxelle. Drape the rest of the spinach over the duxelle, then fold the crêpes up over the beef, and cover it with the unused crêpe (halved if necessary). The beef should now be snugly wrapped.

Lightly brush the short ends of the brioche with egg wash. Fold one long side over the beef, brush with egg wash, then fold the other long side over the top. Roll out the brioche ends and trim to make 3-inch flaps. Brush lightly with egg wash and fold them up over the fillet. Hold a baking sheet at a 45° angle against the side of the brioche-wrapped beef, then tilt and invert the parcel onto the baking sheet with the seam underneath. Refrigerate for 30 minutes.

Preheat the oven to 425°F. Brush the brioche crust with egg wash and use a knife tip to mark a lattice or leaf pattern. Cut a small vent in the middle to let the steam escape during cooking. Bake in the oven, allowing 25 minutes for rare beef, 35 minutes for medium, and 45 minutes for well done. If the brioche crust starts to look too brown during cooking, cover it with parchment paper or foil.

Lift the châteaubriand onto a rack and let rest for 5 minutes, then cut into slices about ¾ inch thick.

pan-fries, sautés, and deep-frying

I offer several pan-fried main course dishes on my restaurant menu. Pan-frying is ideal for cooking small, tender pieces of poultry, fish, and meat, like tournedos, lamb chops, and squab pigeon canoes (page 146). These dishes are cooked *à la minute*, so my customers can order them cooked precisely to their liking, from very rare to well done.

For pan-frying, I use a straight-sided frying pan made from tinned copper or stainless steel with a heavy base, and a little clarified butter or hot (but not smoking) peanut oil. I salt the food just before cooking, but add pepper at the end so it retains its aroma. The food needs to be turned in the pan with tongs (rather than a fork) until it reaches a light golden color; it is sometimes then necessary to partially cover the pan to finish cooking.

Sautéed dishes are cooked uncovered at a higher temperature, and should be fried to a dark nutty brown. Before serving sautéed and pan-fried food, let it rest briefly on a rack while you degrease the pan and deglaze it with a little wine, water, or light stock to make a quick, light flavorful *jus*.

Veal medallions and chops have a tendency to become dry during cooking. To avoid this, first sear them on both sides in a little clarified butter, then throw this away, replace it with fresh butter and finish the cooking over very low heat to keep the meat moist and succulent, especially if you like it pink.

Stir-frying in a wok is one of the fastest cooking methods, which I use to preserve the colors and firm texture of the ingredients, as in my lobster fricassée with peppers (page 144). As it comes into contact with the hot wok, the lobster flesh acquires a light golden crust on the outside, while remaining juicy and moist in the center. A wok is the perfect utensil for cooking lobster, *langoustine*, squid, and vegetables.

When deep-frying, you need to use very fresh oil heated to between 325°F and a maximum of 375°F, depending on what you are frying. A light haze rising from the oil indicates that it is too hot, which can be extremely dangerous, so I strongly recommend that you use a deep-frying thermometer to keep a check on the temperature.

The basic rules for deep-frying are:

• Never fry wet ingredients, or the oil will boil over.

• Fry ingredients in small batches, otherwise the temperature of the oil will drop and the food will absorb too much grease.

• Drain the fried food for a few seconds and place it on paper towels before serving.

• When making French fries, use two pans if possible. Heat the oil in one to 250°F to 265°F, and the other to 347°F. Cook the French fries for 2 to 3 minutes at the lower temperature, then fry in the other pan until crisp and golden.

• Take great care when deep-frying to avoid accidents, and never let children anywhere near the pan.

When the deep-frying oil is cooling and is around 140°F, add a couple of lightly beaten egg whites; these filter the oil and catch any scraps of food. Strain the oil through a fine sieve to use again.

pan-fried skate wings with cherry tomatoes

Blanching skate wings before pan-frying makes them more succulent, and I find the crispy bones at the thin end of the wings utterly divine. Cherry tomatoes are a refreshing alternative to butter or a sauce, or even lemon. Serve with a side salad.

Serves 4

4 skate wings, each about $1/2$ pound, skinned
2 cups milk
2 thyme sprigs
2 bay leaves
3 tablespoons olive oil
1 garlic clove, peeled and thinly sliced
4 clusters of cherry tomatoes on the stem, soaked in cold water for 20 minutes
6 tablespoons clarified butter (page 188)
5 tablespoons cold butter
about 40 small capers, deep-fried for 1 minute
salt and freshly ground pepper

Put the skate wings in a shallow pan and cover with the milk; if necessary, add some cold water to ensure that they are completely immersed. Add the thyme and bay leaves, season lightly, and set over a medium heat. When the liquid has bubbled a few times, take the pan off the heat. Leave the skate wings in the liquid for 3 minutes, then drain and wrap in a well-dampened dish towel.

Preheat the oven to 225°F. Mix the olive oil with the garlic. Drain the tomatoes and brush them generously with the garlicky olive oil. Sprinkle with a little salt, and arrange on a rack set over a baking tray. Cook in the oven for about 20 minutes.

To cook the skate, quickly heat the clarified butter in one or two frying pans. Thoroughly pat dry the skate wings with paper towels, season with salt, and cook in the very hot butter for 3 minutes. Turn them over with a palette knife and cook for another 3 minutes; during this time, lift up the skate wings

slightly and put pieces of cold butter underneath.

To serve, place a skate wing on each plate and sprinkle with fried capers. Arrange a cluster of tomatoes on one side of each wing. Serve at once.

pan-fried monkfish with red pepper confit

The success of this recipe depends on the cooking of the monkfish, which must be precisely timed. The thickness of the medallions will vary according to the size of the monkfish tail from which they have been cut, and this will determine the cooking time. The firm, yet succulent texture of the fish contrasts well with the melting confit peppers.

Serves 4

$1/2$ pound confit sweet red peppers (page 79, about $1/3$ recipe)
4 boneless monkfish medallions, each 6 ounces
6 tablespoons olive oil
few rosemary sprigs
4 garlic cloves, peeled and thinly sliced
2 tablespoons snipped parsley
salt and freshly ground pepper
1 lemon, quartered, to serve

Warm the confit red peppers in their own oil.

Pat the monkfish dry with paper towels and season lightly with salt. Heat the olive oil in a frying pan over a high heat, add the monkfish medallions, and cook for about 2 minutes on each side, depending on their thickness, until golden brown. Halfway through cooking, sprinkle the medallions with rosemary.

To serve, divide the confit peppers between the plates, and arrange a monkfish medallion across them. Add the garlic to the oil remaining in the pan and fry until golden and crisp. Scatter the garlic and parsley over the monkfish and season with pepper. Place a lemon quarter on each plate and serve at once.

lobster fricassée with peppers

This rapid cooking method ensures that the lobster retains all its flavor and wonderful texture. Eat it the moment it is cooked, before the flesh firms up. Serve with rice pilaf or, for a lighter accompaniment, a refreshing stir-fry of bok choy and carrot rounds.

Serves 4

4 live lobsters, just under 1 pound each
2 teaspoons salt
1 teaspoon cayenne pepper
4 tablespoons clarified butter (page 188)
2 green bell peppers, cored, seeded, and thinly sliced
6 tablespoons port wine (preferably white)
rice pilaf (page 93), to serve
24 coriander leaves (cilantro)

PREPARING LIVE LOBSTER

Place the live lobster in a plastic bag in the freezer for 2 hours, then remove from the bag and plunge into a large saucepan of boiling water for 30 seconds.

Twist off the claws, then separate them from the elbow and crack them with a knife blade.

Use the knife tip to separate the head and body.

At the end of the body, just above the tail fin, make an incision with the knife tip on either side of the tail, leaving ⅛ inch in the center of the carapace intact. Hold down the tail fin with your fingers and twist and pull it to separate the body and

extract the intestinal tract. Discard the tract. Using the knife, cut the lobster into 3 chunks, following the line of the articulations.

Cut off two-thirds of the antennae on the head. Split the top of the head shell diagonally for the presentation, lift it off, and scrape out any grit from the inside with the knife tip.

Split the rest of the head, scrape out the coral, remove the membrane, and discard the gritty stomach sac. Cut the edible parts of the head and the legs into pieces to use for the sauce. Put the claws, elbows, tail chunks, and the head shell on a plate. Sprinkle with a mixture of salt and cayenne pepper just before cooking.

Prepare the lobsters (see left). Mix the salt with the cayenne and sprinkle over the lobster pieces.

Heat half the clarified butter in a wok set over a very high heat. Put half the lobster pieces in the wok and cook over the high heat for about 3 minutes, stirring every 20 to 30 seconds, until they are colored and cooked all over.

Scatter over half the peppers, pour on half the port, and continue to cook for 30 seconds, still over a very high heat. Transfer the lobster pieces, except the claws, to a bowl. Cook the claws gently for another minute, then add to the bowl with the cooking juices. Cover with foil and keep warm. Cook the rest of the lobster in the same way.

Using poultry shears, cut off the membrane from under the shell on the lobster chunks. Put a mound of rice pilaf in each of 4 deep plates and place the presentation head shells on top. Arrange the lobster pieces all around and pour the cooking juices over the chunks. Scatter over the coriander leaves and serve at once, with the rice pilaf.

squab pigeon canoes with grape jus

This is an excellent way to serve squab pigeon, or Rock Cornish hens. Pan-frying makes the flesh soft and tender, and the taste is enhanced by the grape-flavored *jus*. Crisp cabbage and melting chestnuts provide contrasts in texture. Most of the preparation can be done in advance; simply pan-fry the birds at the last moment.

Serves 4

4 oven-ready squab pigeons
³/4 cup clarified butter (page 188)
1 carrot, peeled and chopped
1 onion, peeled and chopped
14 ounces seedless white grapes
3 tablespoons sugar
6 tablespoons dry white wine
1 bouquet garni
16 fresh chestnuts, or vacuum-packed peeled chestnuts
1¹/4 cups milk
¹/2 medium Savoy cabbage, cored and thinly shredded
salt and freshly ground pepper

To prepare the squab pigeons, cut off the leg quarters with a knife and set aside. Lift up the skin covering the front of the breasts and remove the wishbones. Keep all the bones to make the *jus*. Using poultry shears, cut the carcasses diagonally, starting below the wings and under the breast fillets. Each squab pigeon will be in two parts: the breasts on the bone with the wings attached (the "canoe") and the back of the carcass. Chop the carcasses; remove any remaining giblets.

To make the *jus*, put 3 tablespoons of the clarified butter in a saucepan with the chopped carcasses, leg bones, and wishbones (and the pigeon necks if you have them). Brown over a medium heat, then lower the heat, add the carrot and onion, and sweat gently for 5 minutes. Tip the contents of the pan into a sieve to get rid of the fat, then return them to the pan.

Set aside 24 of the best grapes for the garnish. Add the rest to the pan, sprinkle with sugar, and cook gently for 5 minutes, stirring occasionally. Deglaze with the wine, reduce it by half, and add enough water to barely cover the bones. Bring to a boil, immediately lower the heat, and skim the surface. Add the bouquet garni and bubble gently for 45 minutes. Pass through a cheesecloth-lined sieve into a small pan and reduce the *jus* to a slightly syrupy consistency. Cover and set aside.

If using fresh chestnuts, heat the broiler to high. Lightly pierce the rounded side of the chestnuts with a small, sharp knife. Place them on a baking sheet and put them under the hot broiler until the shells blister and start to split open. Remove and cover with a dish towel. One at a time, remove the shells and skins with a small, sharp knife. Put the peeled chestnuts in a small saucepan with the milk and cook very gently for about 20 minutes, until tender. Cover the pan and let the chestnuts cool in the milk. Peel and seed the reserved grapes for the garnish.

Heat 5 tablespoons clarified butter in a frying pan. Add the shredded cabbage and cook over a high heat, stirring frequently, until just cooked but still *al dente*. Season with salt and pepper, take off the heat and keep the cabbage warm.

To cook the squab pigeons, season them, and heat the remaining clarified butter in a deep frying pan. Add the breast pieces and cook over a medium heat for 6 to 8 minutes, turning them to color all over. Add the legs and cook in the same way for 8 minutes. The pigeons will now be cooked pink. If you prefer them medium, cook for another 5 minutes. Cover with foil and rest in the pan for a few minutes before serving.

To serve, drain the chestnuts and pour on a little boiling water. Drain thoroughly, making sure you eliminate any milky skin. Put the chestnuts and the reserved grapes in the saucepan containing the *jus*. Heat gently for about 5 minutes, until the *jus* just starts to bubble; immediately remove from the heat.

Pile the cabbage in the middle of 4 plates. Put a squab pigeon breast "canoe" on top of each mound, flanked by the legs. Arrange the chestnuts and grapes around them and sprinkle with a spoonful or two of *jus*. Serve the remaining *jus* separately in a sauce boat.

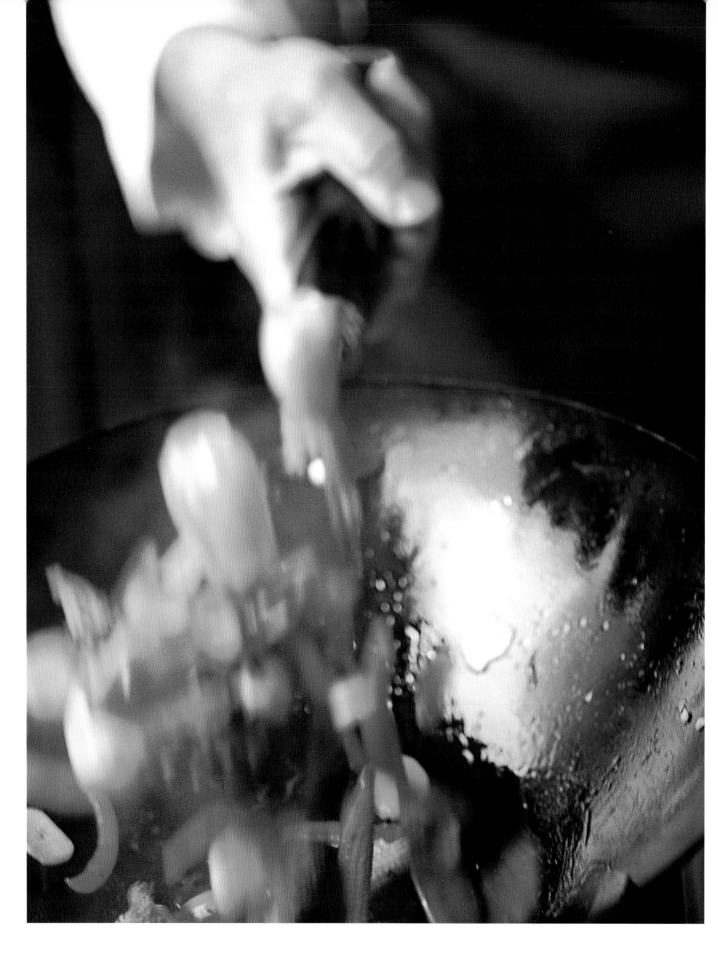

stir-fried vegetables

Stir-frying or "woking" is a very quick method of cooking, in which the colors and flavors of the ingredients remain natural and at their best. Stir-fries not only look and taste delicious, but they are light and healthy, too.

Serves 2

1 tablespoon clarified butter (page 188)

2 carrots, peeled and cut into rounds

4 small bok choy hearts

1 head of broccoli, cut into florets

12 snow peas

1/2 red bell pepper, cored, seeded, and cut into batons

6 ears baby corn, halved lengthwise

2 tablespoons vegetable stock or water

1 garlic clove, finely chopped, or 1 teaspoon grated fresh ginger

1 teaspoon sesame oil

salt

flat-leaf parsley or coriander (cilantro), to garnish

Place the wok over a high heat until smoking, then add the clarified butter.

Add the vegetables to the wok, one variety at a time, starting with the carrots and bok choy. Cook for 30 seconds, stirring continuously with a spatula, or tossing them in the wok with a flick of the wrist. Next, add the broccoli, then the snow peas, still stirring or tossing. Add the red pepper and finally the baby corn.

Season with a little salt, add the vegetable stock or water, and cook for 2 to 3 minutes, according to how crisp you like your vegetables. Add the garlic or ginger and stir-fry briefly. Quickly drizzle over the sesame oil.

Serve garnished with parsley or coriander sprigs.

special pan-fried rib of beef

This is more of a technique than a recipe. Red meat that is pan-fried or roasted conventionally always requires a resting time of 10 to 20 minutes, to allow the flesh to relax and the blood to disperse through it. However, this original method of cooking the meat en papillote before pan-frying allows you to serve it at once, with delicious results. The same method can be applied to a châteaubriand.

I like to serve the beef accompanied with stir-fried vegetables (see left). When cèpes are in season, I sometimes serve a cèpe coulis (page 25) as a treat.

Serves 4

1 rib of beef, about 1³/4 pounds trimmed weight, 2 inches thick

5 tablespoons clarified butter (page 188)

salt and freshly ground pepper

Brush the beef very lightly with clarified butter, then wrap it very tightly in a sheet of foil to make a well-sealed parcel.

Heat a dry frying pan until very hot. Put in the foil-wrapped beef and cook over a medium heat for 3 minutes. Turn it over without piercing the foil, and cook for another 3 minutes.

Remove the beef parcel from the pan, wipe the pan with paper towels, put in the remaining clarified butter, and return it to the heat.

Unwrap the beef, salt it lightly, then put it back in the frying pan. Cook over a medium heat for 7 minutes on each side if you like it rare. If you prefer it medium to well done, cook it for another 5 minutes on each side.

To serve, carve the meat on the diagonal as soon as it is cooked. Place two slices on each plate, grind over a twist of pepper and serve at once.

vegetable tempura

I serve this tempura the moment it comes out of the oil, with curry mayonnaise for dipping.

Serves 6

about 24 slim green beans
12 cauliflower florets, cut into $^1/4$-inch slices
12 broccoli florets, cut into $^1/4$-inch slices
12 mushrooms, halved or quartered, if large
12 baby zucchini with flowers, prepared (see left)
sesame oil (untoasted), or peanut oil, for deep-frying

Tempura batter:

$^1/3$ cup cornstarch
$1^1/3$ cups flour
$^1/2$ teaspoon baking soda
$^1/2$ teaspoon sea salt flakes
$1^3/4$ cups ice-cold, lightly carbonated mineral water (e.g., Badoit or San Pellegrino)

To serve:

curry mayonnaise (page 20)

PREPARING BABY ZUCCHINI WITH FLOWERS

Delicately open up the flower and cut out the stamen with a small sharp knife.

Use the knife to cut out the calyxes that lie at the base of the flower.

Cut the end of the zucchini into a "V" to resemble an arrow tip. Starting at about ¾ inch from the base of the flower, make a series of incisions, cutting through the zucchini at ⅛-inch intervals all along its length, to make a kind of fan. The zucchini is now ready for deep-frying.

Plunge the beans into boiling water and immediately refresh in cold water; drain and pat dry.

To make the batter, put the dry ingredients in a bowl. Mix in the carbonated water a little at a time, stirring with long chopsticks; do not overmix. Don't worry if the batter looks slightly grainy; this is quite normal. Use the batter right away.

Heat the oil in a wok or deep-fat fryer to 325°F to 350°F. Cook the tempura a few at a time, coating each vegetable piece separately. Pick up the vegetable with the long chopsticks, briefly dip into the tempura batter so that it is barely coated, then drop into the hot oil. Repeat with a few more pieces, turning them until golden all over. The tempura are cooked as soon as they rise to the surface; each piece will only take about 1 minute to cook. Remove immediately and drain on paper towels.

Serve at once, with curry mayonnaise for dipping.

langoustine and squid tempura

Seafood such as *langoustines* and squid make superb tempura. Jumbo shrimp, which may be butterflied, are also excellent. I serve the seafood in a bowl, garnished with a few deep-fried parsley sprigs, and accompanied by a bowl of sweet and sour sauce (page 24). Seafood tempura is best eaten with chopsticks.

Serves 6

12 raw langoustines, or jumbo shrimp
12 baby squid
1 quantity tempura batter (see left)
sesame oil (untoasted), or peanut oil, for deep-frying
few deep-fried curly parsley sprigs, to garnish
sweet and sour sauce (page 24), to serve

PREPARING SQUID

Hold the squid body with the fingers of one hand and the tentacles with the other.

Pull the body gently to separate it from the head; remove the soft innards. Cut the triangular fins from the body pouch.

Remove the transparent quill from inside the body pouch.

Peel off the purplish-beige membrane covering the pouch.

Using a knife, slit open the body lengthwise. Lightly score the whole outside surface of the body in a diamond pattern with the tip of the knife.

Press the top of the head between your thumb and index finger to extract the beak. Cut the tentacles from the head. Squeeze the ink sac to extract the black ink, which can be used in sauces, risotto, etc., and is highly prized. (Not all varieties have an ink sac.)

Rinse the pouch, fins, and tentacles in cold water and pat dry before using.

NOTE Similarly, cuttlefish can be prepared in this way. You would need to push out the cuttlebone from the pouch (akin to removing the quill from squid).

Shell the raw *langoustines*, removing the head and legs, but leaving on the last ring of the body shell and the tail. Clean and prepare the squid (see left).

Coat the seafood in the batter and deep-fry in the same way as vegetable tempura (see opposite page), allowing 2 to 3 minutes in the hot oil. Drain on paper towels.

Serve the tempura at once, garnished with deep-fried parsley sprigs, and accompanied by the sweet and sour dipping sauce.

fruit fritters
with saffron
mango coulis

This dessert is a treat for everyone at the table. The only one who suffers is the cook, who has to keep an eye on the oil and fry the fritters a few at a time. That way, they don't go soggy and the guests enjoy them all the more.

Serves 6

1 1/4 pounds firm, ripe fruits (strawberries, cherries, small pineapple, apple, banana, apricots, pears, etc.)
1/4 cup sugar
juice of 1 lemon
4 tablespoons kirsch (optional)
oil for deep-frying

Batter:

1/4 ounce compressed yeast (about 1/2 cake), or 1 rounded teaspoon active dry yeast (about 1/2 package)
5 tablespoons milk
1 cup less 1 tablespoon flour
pinch of salt
1 egg yolk
4 tablespoons beer
2 tablespoons peanut oil
1 1/2 egg whites (scant 1/4 cup)
1/4 cup sugar

To serve:

sugar, for sprinkling
saffron mango coulis (page 28)

First make the batter. In a bowl, dissolve the yeast in half the milk. Put the flour and salt in a mixing bowl and slowly pour in the rest of the milk, whisking continuously. Add the egg yolk and beer, still whisking. When everything is well amalgamated, add the yeast mixture and the peanut oil. Mix thoroughly with the whisk. Cover the bowl with plastic wrap and let the batter stand at room temperature for 2 hours.

Peel the fruits and prepare them according to size. Leave strawberries and cherries whole. Slice and core pineapple. Cut the other fruits into quarters or slices, discarding pits and cores.

Put the fruits in a bowl with the sugar, lemon juice, and kirsch, if using. Let marinate for 30 minutes.

To cook the fritters, heat the oil for deep-frying to about 350°F. To finish the batter, beat the egg whites until half-risen, then add the sugar and beat until firm. Fold delicately into the batter.

Cook the fritters a few at a time. Using a fork and your fingertips, dip the fruits one by one into the batter, making sure they are well coated, then drop them, one at a time, into the hot oil and fry for 1 to 3 minutes, depending on their size, until pale golden. As the fritters rise to the surface, turn them over with a fork so that the whole surface is colored. Remove and drain on paper towels. Cook all the fritters in the same way.

To serve, put a crown of green pineapple leaves in the middle of a serving plate and arrange the fritters around it. Sprinkle with sugar, as generously as you like. Serve the mango coulis separately.

casseroles and slow-cooking

These slow-cooked dishes are my favorites in the winter months. They carry the flame of French bourgeois cooking – the product of our countryside. They are the dishes our mothers cooked when we were children – made without much money, but plenty of love. Those were the days ...

I have chosen to modify the recipes without compromising or turning my back on excellent old-fashioned, gentle, slow-cooking methods, which are best suited to humble cuts of beef, lamb, veal,

and meat from other cloven-hoofed animals. I have created a blanquette of lamb (page 162), adding mint to make a refreshing, light dish that does not use egg yolks to thicken the sauce; and my modern version of veal carbonnade (page 167) has a light, tasty *jus* and a colorful garnish of vegetables that marries well with the flavors of the veal. Ragoûts of poultry and game are also deliciously tender and tasty cooked in a casserole with very little liquid.

None of these cooking methods will tolerate an oven temperature higher than 325°F. If you cook on a gas stove, it is essential to use a heat diffuser to keep the temperature at or below 175°F to ensure that the meat becomes tender.

When it comes to fish, particularly salmon, turbot, carp, trout, and monkfish, I prefer to braise them in the oven, either whole or cut into large pieces on the bone. I baste them frequently with a little

liquid flavored with a touch of fresh ginger, saffron, vanilla, or curry. When the fish is cooked, I add a squeeze of lemon juice and a knob of butter to the cooking juices, to make a sauce that is glossy and smooth on the palate, then serve this separately in a sauce boat.

In winter, I have a passion for classic cassoulet topped with a layer of chopped pork rinds and fresh bread crumbs mixed with parsley, which form a delicious thick crust. I have overstuffed myself more than once with this dish, which is *oh so* delicious, but too rich. I can't bear to forgo the pleasure of eating it, so I have resolved to lighten the recipe by replacing the pork and lamb with confit shoulders of rabbit. They are more digestible and add an original twist to this French classic (see recipe on page 164).

In summer, I love tagines, the succulent stews so popular in Morocco. I prefer vegetable tagines, to which I add some fresh herbs from the garden at the end of cooking. Garlic and onions are vital ingredients, adding their special aromas to the vegetables as they cook gently in olive oil – like a fruit compote simmering in its syrup.

Mastering the technique for slow-cooked dishes is easy. All you need is a little time and patience, since they require an hour or two's cooking. Always make sure that the ingredients are not swimming in liquid, but just resting on a bed of red or white wine, beer, light vegetable, chicken, or fish stock, or simply water – you can't fail! Most of these dishes will freeze very well and can be successfully reheated in a microwave, so I recommend that you prepare them for six to ten people, then divide them into smaller portions and freeze them in airtight containers to use another time.

vegetable tagine with fish fillets

Vegetable tagine is one of the most ubiquitous dishes in Morocco. In Tunisia, they add fish caught by the local fishermen; I like to use red mullet from the Mediterranean but you can use any firm-fleshed lean fish. You can substitute different vegetables for those listed; just be sure to start with those that need the longest cooking and finish with the most delicate. If possible, cook the dish in an earthenware tagine, about 12 inches in diameter; if you haven't got one, use a heavy casserole instead.

Serves 6

3 fennel bulbs, cut lengthwise into slices
about 5/8 inch thick
3 bell peppers, preferably one each red, yellow,
and green, halved, cored, and seeded
3/4 cup olive oil
12 white button onions, peeled
6 unpeeled garlic cloves
3 small eggplants, cut into thick batons
3 zucchini, cut into large almond shapes
12 medium cherry tomatoes
2 thyme sprigs
1 savory sprig
24 fava beans, preferably fresh, skinned
6 red mullet or other firm-fleshed lean fish fillets,
about 6 ounces each
salt and freshly ground pepper
coriander (cilantro) leaves, to garnish

First prepare the vegetables. Blanch the fennel in boiling water, refresh in cold water, and drain. Cut the peppers into 1¼-inch squares.

Pour one-third of the olive oil into the tagine or casserole. Place on a medium heat, using a heat diffuser if the tagine has an earthenware base (which must not be placed directly on a naked flame). Add the onions and sweat over a medium heat for 5 minutes.

Add the garlic and peppers and cook for 10 minutes, stirring from time to time, to bring the vegetables into the middle of the tagine.

Add the eggplant and blanched fennel. Add a little salt and pour another third of the oil over the vegetables. Cover the tagine with its conical "hat" or place the lid on the casserole. Let simmer gently over medium heat for 15 minutes.

The vegetables will now be half cooked and becoming tender. Stir gently, bringing them into the middle of the tagine, then add the zucchini, tomatoes, thyme, savory, and all but 2 tablespoons of the remaining oil. Cover and cook for another 30 to 40 minutes on the heat diffuser set over a very low heat, or in the oven at 325°F, until the vegetables are done to your liking.

Scatter on the fava beans. Season the fish fillets with salt and pepper, arrange them on top of the vegetables, and sprinkle with the remaining olive oil. Replace the lid and simmer for another 7 to 8 minutes, until the fish is cooked.

To serve, just put the tagine in the middle of the table and lift the lid so that your guests can enjoy the aromas of the vegetables and fish as they waft out, and appreciate the mosaic effect of the different colors. Scatter on some coriander leaves and serve.

pheasant en cocotte

This dish, complete with its elaborate garnishes, takes time to prepare, but much of the preparation can be done in advance, so it is ideal for a special occasion. Cooking pheasants en cocotte ensures that they remain succulent, and cooking the thighs separately in parcels adds a gourmet touch. Of course, you can simplify the dish by cutting the pheasants into portions and omitting the more elaborate garnishes. Pig's caul may be ordered from some specialist butchers.

Serves 4

2 plump oven-ready pheasants, about
1³/4 pounds each
1¹/4 cups sweet hard cider
9 tablespoons clarified butter (page 188)
1 carrot, peeled and chopped
1 onion, peeled and chopped
1 bouquet garni
6 juniper berries, lightly crushed
salt and freshly ground pepper

Stuffing:

2 slices crustless white bread, finely diced and
soaked in 6 tablespoons milk
1 cup finely chopped button mushrooms
¹/2 cup finely chopped shallots
¹/2 cup chopped parsley
1 egg, beaten
3¹/2 ounces pig's caul (if available)
16 attractive flat-leaf parsley leaves

Garnishes:

2 apples, preferably Reinette or Granny Smith
confectioners' sugar, to glaze
8 shallots, peeled
6 tablespoons peanut oil
2 pinches of sugar
1 tablespoon wine vinegar
1 small pear, preferably Bartlett or
Louise Bonne d'Avranches
small bunch of watercress

To prepare the pheasants, cut off the leg quarters. Lift up the skin covering the front of the breasts, remove the wishbones with the tip of a knife, and set aside. Using poultry shears, cut the carcasses diagonally, starting below the wings and under the breast fillets. This will cut each pheasant into two parts: the breasts on the bone with the wings attached; and the back of the carcass. Chop the carcass backs; set aside.

Next, prepare the stuffing parcels. Remove the skin from the pheasant thighs and cut off the flesh. Keep the drumsticks and thigh bones for the sauce. Trim off the fat and sinews. Cut the flesh into tiny dice and place in a bowl. Drain and lightly press the bread; add to the bowl with the mushrooms, shallots, and parsley; stir well. Mix in the egg. Season this stuffing lightly with salt and pepper.

Spread the caul on a work surface and lay 8 parsley leaves on it, spaced well apart. Put a large spoonful of stuffing on each leaf and top with another parsley leaf. Cut the caul around each heap of stuffing and wrap to enclose it. (Alternatively, save the parsley leaves to garnish and shape the stuffing into small patties.) Put the stuffing parcels on a plate, cover with plastic wrap and refrigerate until ready to use.

For the apple garnish, cut each apple vertically into three pieces. Keep the central core section for the sauce. Lay the rounded pieces cut-side down on the work surface. Cut out rounds with a 2-inch fluted pastry cutter and peel the tops. Using a small melon baller, cut out a ball from the middle of each slice. Replace the apple ball in the hollow, turning it so the inner surface now faces outwards to make a "nipple."

Preheat the broiler to very hot. Put the 4 fluted apple slices in a small, deep, heatproof dish, moisten with 3 tablespoons of the cider, and sprinkle with a generous pinch of confectioners' sugar. Broil for 12 to 15 minutes, basting them with the juices every 3 or 4 minutes once the sugar has melted. The apples should be lightly caramelized and just cooked in the middle. Take them out of the cider; keep warm.

Now make the sauce. Heat 2½ tablespoons clarified butter in a saucepan, add the chopped carcass backs, thigh bones, drumsticks, and wishbones, and color them over a medium heat. Add the carrot, onion, and reserved apple core sections. Simmer over a low heat for 5 minutes, then tip the contents of the pan into a colander to drain off the fat; return to the saucepan. Deglaze with the remaining cider and reduce it by half, then add enough cold water just to cover the bones. Bring to a boil, lower the heat, and skim the surface. Add the bouquet garni and juniper berries, and simmer gently for 45 minutes. Strain through a fine conical sieve, return the sauce to the pan, and reduce to a slightly syrupy consistency. Season to taste, pour into a bowl, and keep covered.

Put the shallots in a small saucepan with the peanut oil and cook them at 160°F to 175°F for 10 minutes. Drain the shallots, put them into a small frying pan with 1 tablespoon clarified butter and a pinch of sugar, and brown them over a high heat. Deglaze the pan with 1 tablespoon wine vinegar, season with salt and pepper to taste, and add the shallots to the apples; keep warm.

Heat 1 tablespoon clarified butter in a small frying pan and sprinkle on a pinch of sugar. Quarter the pear, add to the pan, and cook until golden on both sides. Keep warm with the apples and shallots.

To cook the pheasant breasts, season them with salt, heat 2½ tablespoons clarified butter in a casserole, and brown the pheasant on all sides for 6 to 8 minutes. Cover the casserole and cook very gently on a heat diffuser for another 15 minutes. Take the breasts out of the casserole, cover with foil, and rest for 10 minutes.

Meanwhile, heat 2 tablespoons clarified butter in a frying pan, add the stuffing parcels, and cook over a medium heat for 2 to 3 minutes on each side.

To serve, reheat the sauce. Take the pheasant breasts off the bone and cut each into three. Stand the breastbones upright on plates and reconstitute the breasts, placing the meat in its original position. Arrange the glazed apples, pears, shallots, and stuffing parcels around the pheasant, and pop a few watercress leaves in between. Serve the sauce separately in a sauce boat.

blanquette of lamb with mint and a fine egg crust

Simple, light, and refreshing, this modern version of a blanquette can be prepared a day in advance and reheated gently on the stove or in a *bain-marie*. Serve with a rice pilaf (page 93), or plain boiled rice with some golden raisins added.

Serves 6

2 boned shoulders of lamb, about 3¹/₄ pounds total boned weight
4 medium carrots, peeled and cut into thick rounds
2 medium onions, peeled and stuck with 6 cloves
1 bouquet garni
1 bunch of mint, about 3¹/₂ ounces, plus ¹/₄ cup snipped mint leaves
3 tablespoons butter, at room temperature
¹/₄ cup flour
6 tablespoons heavy cream
14 ounces broccoli florets, steamed until crisp
salt and freshly ground pepper

Egg and herb crust:

4 hard-boiled eggs, coarsely chopped
¹/₃ cup finely snipped flat-leaf parsley
¹/₄ cup finely snipped mint leaves

Trim the lamb, removing all sinews and fat, and cut into 1½-inch cubes. Place in a shallow saucepan, cover generously with cold water and set over a high heat. The moment the water comes to a boil, lower the heat and continue to cook very gently for 10 minutes; the temperature must not exceed 160°F.

Add the carrots, onions, bouquet garni, and a little salt. Continue to cook at 160°F for 1¹/₂ hours, skimming the surface as necessary. By this time, the meat should be tender and perfectly cooked.

Add the bunch of mint and cook for another 10 minutes, at the same temperature. Lift out the lamb and put into a deep dish; cover with a very damp cloth.

Mash together the butter and flour to make a paste (beurre manié). Strain the cooking liquid through a conical sieve into a saucepan, discarding the carrots, onions, mint, and bouquet garni. Bring the liquid to a boil and reduce by one-quarter, then whisk in the paste, a small piece at a time. Cook over a medium heat for about 10 minutes, whisking continuously to make a very light velouté. Add the cream and bubble the sauce for 3 minutes, still whisking.

Strain the sauce through a fine conical sieve onto the lamb. Mix carefully, then add the snipped mint leaves. Transfer to a flameproof casserole, add the broccoli, and season with salt and pepper. Keep the blanquette warm on a heat diffuser over a very low heat, or in a *bain-marie*.

To serve, mix the chopped eggs with the snipped parsley and mint. Spoon the blanquette into shallow bowls or individual gratin dishes, sprinkle the egg crust over the surface and serve at once.

chicken cooked in a sealed cocotte with riesling and girolles

I have adapted this rustic dish to give it a lighter, more modern touch. During the slow cooking, the girolles are almost melted on the pieces of chicken, and the *jus* is mild and sweet. Fresh fettuccine (page 84), tossed with fine slivers of lemon zest, is the ideal accompaniment.

I always use a fine quality medium-dry Riesling when cooking this recipe. The house of Beyer in Alsace is renowned for its excellent Riesling, which is available from good wine merchants. Of course, as soon as I open the bottle, I have to sip half a glassful to check that it isn't corked.

Serves 4

1 very plump free-range chicken, about 4 pounds, cut into 8 pieces
4 tablespoons clarified butter (page 188)
16 baby white onions, peeled
10 ounces carrots, peeled and cut into chunky sticks
1 bottle of Riesling wine
5 tablespoons butter
1 1/2 pounds girolles, cleaned, or other (preferably wild) mushrooms
1 1/4 cups flour, to seal the lid
salt and freshly ground pepper

Season the chicken pieces with salt and pepper. Put the clarified butter in a lidded cast-iron casserole and set over a medium heat. When the butter is hot, add the chicken pieces and cook, turning them over after a few minutes, until they are evenly colored all over.

Remove the chicken breast pieces, add the onions to the casserole, and cook with the leg pieces for about 7 minutes longer. Remove the leg pieces, pour off most of the fat from the casserole, add the carrots and Riesling, and cook gently until the liquid has reduced by three-quarters.

Preheat the oven to 350°F. Heat the butter in a frying pan over a medium heat, add the girolles, and cook until they render their liquid. Tip them into a colander, drain well, and season lightly with salt. Return all the chicken pieces to the casserole, add the girolles, and put on the lid.

Put the flour in a bowl and add a little cold water, stirring with a spoon to make a softish paste. Use the spoon to spread this paste between the edge of the lid and the outside top edge of the casserole to create a hermetic seal. Cook in the oven for 20 minutes.

To serve, bring the casserole to the table. Break the seal and lift off the lid so that all the aromas of this marvelous chicken dish waft out for the pleasure of your guests.

cassoulet of rabbit confit

In this modern cassoulet, the beans are simply cooked in water, which accentuates their flavor and makes the dish very light. The best dried beans come from Cazères, Pamiers, and Tarbes; buy these if you can and soak them in cold water for 6 hours beforehand. If you are using ordinary white beans, such as Great Northern or navy, you will need to soak them for 12 hours. The rabbit confit gives this classic dish an unusual twist.

Serves 4

2¹/₂ cups dried white beans, soaked overnight (see above)
1 onion, stuck with a clove
1 large carrot, peeled and cut into 4 chunks
1 bouquet garni
1 small smoked sausage (preferably Morteaux or Montbéliard)
2 long chipolatas or spicy pork sausages
1 tablespoon peanut oil
4 confit rabbit shoulders (page 80)
4 thick slices of garlic sausage or Kielbasa
6 tablespoons fresh bread crumbs
2 tablespoons chopped flat-leaf parsley
salt and freshly ground pepper

Drain the beans and put into a saucepan with the onion, carrot, and bouquet garni. Cover generously with cold water and bring to a boil over a medium heat. Bubble gently for 10 minutes, then lower the heat, skim the surface, and simmer very gently for about 1½ hours.

Blanch the smoked sausage in boiling water, refresh in cold water, and add it to the beans. Cook for a another 30 minutes, or until the beans are tender. When they are, turn off the heat and season lightly with salt, and more generously with pepper.

Blanch the chipolata sausages in boiling water, refresh in cold water, and drain well; set aside.

Heat the oil in a frying pan, add the rabbit, and fry over a medium heat until golden all over. Transfer them to a plate. Add the chipolatas to the pan and fry in the same way.

When you are ready to serve the cassoulet, preheat the oven to 400°F. Halve the chipolatas and cut the smoked sausage into 8 slices. Remove the onion, carrot, and bouquet garni from the beans. Divide the beans between individual deep ovenproof china or earthenware bowls. To each bowl, add a shoulder of rabbit, half a chipolata, two slices of smoked sausage, and a slice of garlic sausage. Place the bowls in the hot oven for 5 minutes.

Mix together the bread crumbs and parsley, sprinkle the mixture over the cassoulet, and return the bowls to the oven for 5 minutes. Serve at once.

cassoulet of pork chops with confit tomatoes

Replace the rabbit with thin pork rib chops or cutlets. Prepare the cassoulet as above and pan-fry the pork (as for the rabbit) until lightly and evenly colored.

Add to the cooked beans and simmer for 5 minutes, then add a few confit tomatoes (page 79), and continue as above.

carbonnade of veal with baby carrots and fava beans

This classic dish is traditionally made with beef, but I prefer to use veal, which is more delicate and makes a lighter carbonnade, better suited to my modern style of cooking. The beet adds a brilliant touch of purple, which runs into the sauce without altering its character, and its sweet, slightly acidic taste reinforces the flavor of the veal.

Serves 4

2¹/4 pounds boneless veal loin or rib roast (boned rack of veal)

5 tablespoons clarified butter (page 188)

2 medium onions, peeled and diced

2 large carrots, peeled and sliced

¹/2 pound tomatoes, peeled, seeded, and chopped

2 cups dry white wine

1²/3 cups boiling veal stock or water

1 medium bouquet garni

24 baby carrots, with their tops, scrubbed and blanched

14 ounces fava beans (weight in the pod), shelled, skinned, and blanched

1 beet, about 5 ounces, half-cooked until still firm, and peeled

salt and freshly ground pepper

Preheat the oven to 285°F. Cut the veal into 8 equal slices, and season lightly with salt. Put half the clarified butter in a frying pan and set over a high heat. Put in 4 slices of veal, and color for 2 to 3 minutes on each side. Transfer them to an ovenproof casserole with a lid. Repeat with the other 4 slices of veal.

In the same frying pan, sweat the onions and sliced carrots over a medium heat for 5 minutes. Add the tomatoes and cook for another 5 minutes. Pour the wine into the pan and cook until it has reduced by two-thirds.

Pour the contents of the pan into the casserole, and add the boiling veal stock or water and the bouquet garni. Cover and cook in the oven for 1³/4 to 2 hours. The temperature inside the casserole should not exceed 175°F during this time. Press a slice of veal with your fingertips to check whether it is cooked; it should feel tender and flexible. Gently transfer the veal slices to a shallow flameproof porcelain dish, being careful not to break them. Cover the dish with plastic wrap, and keep warm.

Strain the cooking liquid into a saucepan, set over a low heat, and reduce to the slightly syrupy consistency of a light *jus*. Check the seasoning. Add the whole carrots and simmer for 5 minutes, until they are cooked but still firm. Finally, add the fava beans and cook for another 1 minute. Pour the *jus*, carrots, and fava beans over the veal, place the dish on a heat diffuser, and simmer gently for 2 to 3 minutes.

Serve the carbonnade straight from the porcelain dish, or in individual deep plates. Coarsely grate the beet over the top just before serving.

baking

This type of cooking evokes fond memories of my apprenticeship when, at the age of fourteen, I learned to handle the baker's shovel in a three-tier oven; it was 10 feet long – twice my own height! The temperature of each tier was different to enable the *pâtissier* to bake a whole range of cakes and baked goods. Certain pastries require an oven temperature of 325ºF, while others need to be cooked at 475ºF; the 575ºF hottest oven at the bottom, which we called "lethal," was only used for glazing pithiviers, millefeuilles, and the like. The heat it

emitted was so intense that I only had 3 or 4 seconds to thrust in my shovel laden with pastries dusted with confectioners' sugar, and hastily pull it out again before they got burned – a fascinating experience for a young chef! During the Epiphany period, I had to bake more than 500 *galettes des rois* (Twelfth night cakes) in the space of 3 or 4 days, in addition to the regular daily orders. I was proud of my position as oven-minder; it is a key job, which demands an almost innate skill and a good deal of attention and discipline. Baked goods must be carefully watched; the oven can heat, dry, and cook, but unfortunately, it can also burn – and all too often it does. That is why I always recommend using a kitchen timer.

Although this chapter is largely based on classic doughs and pastries – savory and sweet pastry dough, puff pastry, and brioche – I have included a number of original creations, like my crab and rice

noodle quiche (page 174), with its subtle flavors and textures, and my croustade with vegetable "spaghetti" (page 173), which includes seaweed to enhance the taste of the vegetables. Baked macaroons are delectable served with coffee, and I enjoy developing interesting new flavor variations; my customers at The Waterside Inn adore my novel cinnamon macaroons (page 185).

The step-by-step photographs on page 171 show you exactly how to assemble my tempting anchovy straws, which I can't resist nibbling straight from the oven, at the risk of burning myself in the process ... These *amuse-gueules* are simple to make if you follow the instructions. The anchovies can be replaced with pitted olives, which go equally well with the pastry; better still, delight your guests with a harmonious arrangement of both varieties.

As baking is a process of cooking with dry heat – without liquid or fat – the goods are baked in molds or directly on a baking sheet. We bake bread, rolls, tarts, pizzas, pâtés en croûte, and all sorts of small cakes and pastries. Do try my little barquettes (page 178), which are cooled then filled with crème Chantilly and chocolate ganache, to delicious effect.

An oven is a piece of equipment that is in constant use, and it must be cleaned regularly, especially after cooking onions, garlic, fish, or anything that spatters grease. Cleaning will prevent the oven from smoking and ensure that your delicate macaroons or brioche are not contaminated by strong, inappropriate flavors. I recommend that you invest in a self-cleaning oven to avoid such pitfalls. One must move with the times for high performance cooking.

rough puff pastry

This puff pastry is very quick and easy to make. You will be amazed at how it rises when it is cooked – almost as much as classic puff pastry. I use it to make anchovy straws (see right), and croustade with vegetable "spaghetti" (page 173).

Makes about 2½ pounds

3¹/₃ cups (1 pound) all-purpose flour, or
²/₃ cup cake flour and 2²/₃ cups all-purpose
flour, plus extra for dusting
1 pound (4 sticks) well-chilled unsalted butter,
cut into small cubes
1¹/₂ teaspoons fine salt
³/₄ cup ice water

Put the flour in a mound on the work surface, make a well in the center, and add the cubes of butter and salt. Using your fingertips, work the butter and flour together, gradually drawing the flour into the middle.

When the butter cubes are half-squashed and the dough is becoming grainy, pour in the ice water in a steady stream, mixing with your other hand.

Continue to mix the dough with your fingertips until all the water is incorporated.

Then gather the dough and knead it several times by pushing it away from you with the heel of your hand. It should be fairly smooth, but you will still see some small particles of butter. Shape the dough into a ball, wrap in plastic wrap, and refrigerate for 15 minutes, to relax the dough and chill the butter.

Lightly flour the work surface and roll out the pastry into a 12- x 6-inch rectangle. Fold this rectangle into three. This is called the first turn.

Give the block of pastry a quarter-turn, then roll it out as before, and fold into three. This is the second turn. Lightly press two fingertips into the block to remind yourself that you have made two turns. Wrap the pastry in plastic wrap and refrigerate for 20 minutes.

Give the chilled pastry two more turns, rolling and folding as before. Wrap and refrigerate for at least 30 minutes, or up to 3 days until ready to use.

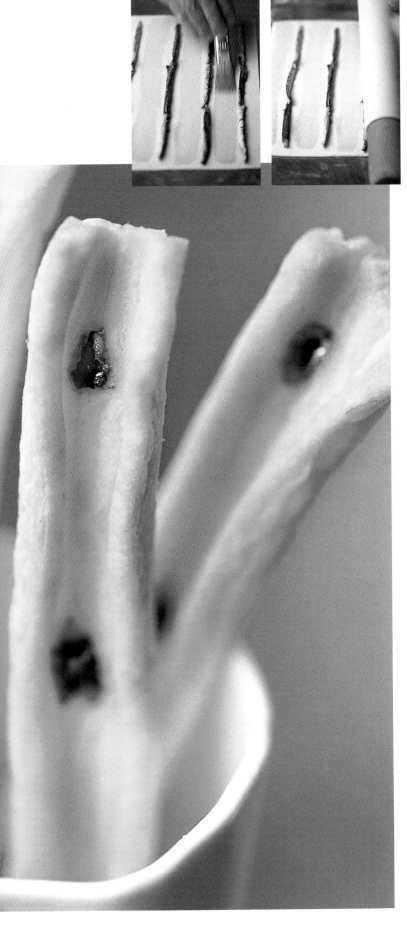

anchovy straws

These flaky straws are best served warm from the oven – with apéritifs or consommé. Stuffed olives, laid end to end, can replace the anchovies, though the straws won't be as streamlined.

Serves 8

3/4 pound rough puff pastry (see left)
flour, for dusting
20 anchovy fillets canned in oil
1 egg yolk mixed with 1 tablespoon milk (egg wash)

Lightly flour the work surface and roll out the pastry into a rectangle ⅛ inch thick. Halve the rectangle lengthwise, wrap one half, and keep in the fridge.

If the anchovies are too thick, halve them lengthwise. Starting ¾ inch in from the edge of the pastry, lay a line of anchovies along the length of the rectangle. Repeat to make 3 more lines, leaving a scant 1 inch of space between each one. Brush the exposed pastry between the anchovies with egg wash.

Take the other piece of pastry from the fridge, lift it on the rolling pin, and lay it over the first pastry sheet.

Press firmly with your fingertips to seal, taking care not to press down on the anchovies. Chill in the fridge for 20 minutes.

Preheat the oven to 400°F. Trim and neaten the pastry edges, then cut the pastry rectangle crosswise into long strips, ⅛ inch wide. The pastry strips will be dotted with anchovy pieces. As you cut the anchovy straws, place them on a baking sheet, flat-side down. Bake in the hot oven for 5 to 6 minutes. If the straws in the corners of the baking sheet are cooked before the rest, just lift them off with a palette knife so that they do not burn. Cool on a wire rack.

croustade with vegetable "spaghetti"

This dish is perfect for vegetarians, and you can vary it by using different vegetables. To make the "spaghetti" the vegetables need to be at least 5 inches long, and cooked until crunchy to keep their shape. Try to include seaweed, which enhances the flavor of the other vegetables. Thanks to the astonishing way rough puff pastry rises, the croustade will be at least 2 inches high.

Serves 4

1 1/2 pounds rough puff pastry (page 170)
flour, for dusting
1 egg yolk mixed with 1 tablespoon milk (egg wash)
3 1/2 ounces fresh or preserved spaghetti seaweed (optional)
1 cucumber
1 butternut squash
1 daikon (white radish)
1 carrot
2 zucchini
1 tablespoon peanut oil
4 small cherry tomatoes
1 1/4 cups sauce suprême (page 18), made with vegetable stock
salt and freshly ground pepper

Preheat the oven to 425°F. Roll out the pastry on a lightly floured surface into a 6½- to 7-inch square, about ¼ inch thick. Place on a baking sheet and chill in the fridge for at least 30 minutes.

Place the chilled pastry square on the work surface and trim the edges with a heavy cook's knife, to make a neat square. Cut a strip about ½ inch wide from each side, taking care to maintain the shape. Slide a palette knife under the square and carefully lift onto the baking sheet. Brush the surface with egg wash, then place a pastry strip along one side of the square, and brush it with egg wash. Repeat on the other 3 sides, positioning and brushing one pastry strip at a time.

Using a knife blade, make a series of light vertical cuts, about ½ inch apart, along the sides of the square, to help the pastry rise as it cooks. With the knife tip, lightly score the raised edges diagonally and score criss-crosses on the corners. Mark leaf shapes in the center of the pastry, which will become the lid, and prick this in two places with the knife tip.

Bake in the hot oven for 10 minutes, then lower the setting to 400°F. Bake for another 30 minutes, covering the croustade loosely with foil or parchment paper if it is browning too quickly.

Using a palette knife, transfer the croustade to a wire rack. Run a knife tip between the lid and the raised edges to a depth of ½ inch, to cut around the lid. Slide the knife under the lid and delicately lift it.

Meanwhile, prepare the vegetable "spaghetti." Rinse the seaweed, if using, thoroughly in cold water for several minutes, especially if it has been preserved in salt. Blanch in boiling water for 1 minute, refresh in cold water, drain, and set aside.

Peel the cucumber and, using a mandoline slicer, cut the flesh into long julienne, but don't include the seeds in the middle. Blanch for 15 seconds, refresh, and drain. Prepare and blanch the squash in the same way, avoiding the soft central part. Repeat with the daikon, using the whole vegetable. Do the same with the carrot, avoiding the woody center, but blanch it for 1½ minutes; refresh and drain.

Wash the zucchini but do not peel. Cut the bright green skin into julienne with the mandoline; don't use the flesh. Blanch for 15 seconds, refresh, and drain.

Heat the oil in a small frying pan, put in the tomatoes and color them for barely 2 minutes. Heat the sauce in a *bain-marie* and let it bubble for 1 minute just before serving.

Place the croustade on a flat serving plate. Carefully mix all the vegetable "spaghetti" together, put them in a colander, and plunge into boiling water for 15 seconds. Drain well and tip into a warmed bowl. Pour over two-thirds of the sauce, mix carefully with a large fork and season to taste. Fill the croustade with the vegetables and place a tomato at each corner. Balance the pastry lid on top and serve the rest of the sauce separately in a sauce boat.

pâte brisée

This light, short pastry dough, with its delicate texture, is one of my favorites. It is used for quiches and tarts, such as crab and rice noodle quiche (see right) and salmon mousse and spinach tartlets (page 70). I also use it for fish, meat, and pâtés en croûte, like my wild boar and morel pâté en croûte (page 73).

Makes about 1 pound

1³/4 cups (9 ounces) all-purpose flour, or ¹/2 cup cake flour and 1¹/4 cups all-purpose flour, plus more for dusting
6 ounces (1¹/2 sticks) unsalted butter, cut into small pieces
1 egg
1 teaspoon fine salt
pinch of sugar
1 tablespoon cold milk

Put the flour in a mound on the work surface and make a well in the center. Put in all the other ingredients, except the milk. Using the fingertips of one hand, mix these ingredients, drawing in the flour, a little at a time, with your other hand. When the dough is almost amalgamated, incorporate the milk.

Lightly flour the work surface and knead the dough 2 or 3 times by pushing it away from you with the heel of your hand. It should be smooth and pliable. Wrap it in parchment paper or plastic wrap and keep in the fridge until ready to use.

NOTE: French flour is milled from softer wheat with less gluten. Using a proportion of cake flour with all-purpose flour produces similar results.

crab and rice noodle quiche

This unusual quiche is creamy without being too rich. It is best served warm, rather than piping hot, to appreciate the delicate flavor of the crab, with a side salad of peppery aragula leaves. You will need a tart pan, about 1½ inches deep.

Serves 8 to 10

1 crab, about 4¹/2 pounds, preferably live, or 10 ounces fresh white crab meat
10 ounces pâte brisée (see left)
flour, for dusting
1 egg yolk mixed with 1 tablespoon milk (egg wash)
1 ounce rice noodles (about 1 cup, broken)
1 teaspoon English mustard powder
1 cup milk
²/3 cup plus 1 tablespoon heavy cream
3 eggs, plus 2 yolks
salt and cayenne pepper
12 coriander leaves (cilantro)

If using a live crab, scrub lightly to remove any silt from the shell, then plunge into a pan of lightly salted water and cook for 10 minutes. Turn off the heat and leave the crab in the water for 20 minutes, then take it out, and let cool for at least 1 hour.

When the crab is cold, break off the legs and claws, lift off the top carapace, scrape out and set aside all the white meat, taking care to pick out any bits of shell and cartilage. You should have about 10 ounces of white meat. Scrape out any roe or firmish brown meat from the carapace and keep it in a bowl.

Roll out the pastry on a lightly floured surface to a thickness of ¹/8 inch and use to line a greased, deep 8-inch removeable-bottom tart pan. Chill the pastry shell in the fridge for 20 minutes.

Preheat the oven to 400°F. Prick the chilled pastry shell in several places with a fork. Line it with parchment paper or foil, then fill with dried or ceramic baking beans. Bake for 20 minutes, then remove the beans, and paper or foil. Lightly brush the pastry base with egg wash and return to the oven for 3 minutes.

Put the rice noodles in a bowl and cover with lightly salted boiling water. Soak for 15 minutes, then drain, refresh, and pat dry with a dish towel. Cut the noodles into 2-inch lengths and mix gently with the white crab.

Put the mustard powder in a bowl and pour on the milk, whisking continuously until blended. Whisk in the cream, eggs, and egg yolks, and season with salt and cayenne pepper.

When ready to bake, set the oven to 340°F. Half-fill the pastry shell with the crab meat and noodle mixture, and scatter small pieces of roe or dark crab meat, if any, on top. Fill up with white meat and noodles. Arrange the coriander leaves on top, pushing them down lightly. Finally, pour in the filling mixture.

Bake the quiche for 1 to 1¼ hours, until a fine knife tip inserted into the center comes out clean. Remove the edge of the pan and slide the quiche onto a wire rack. Leave until warm or tepid before serving.

pâte sucrée

This sweetened pastry dough makes an excellent base for sweet tarts and tartlets. I use it for my caramelized melon and macaroon tart (page 181) and ganache barquettes with crème Chantilly (see right). You can also shape it into small cookies to serve as petits fours. It can be stored for several days in the fridge, or frozen for at least a month.

Makes about 1¼ pounds

1³/4 cups (9 ounces) all-purpose flour, or ¹/2 cup
cake flour and 1¹/4 cups all-purpose flour
7 tablespoons unsalted butter, cubed and slightly
softened
¹/2 cup confectioners' sugar, sifted
small pinch of salt
2 eggs, at room temperature

Put the flour in a mound on the work surface and make a well in the center. Put the butter, confectioners' sugar, and salt in the well, and mix these ingredients together thoroughly with the fingertips of one hand. Add the eggs, and mix again. Using your other hand, gradually draw the flour into the center to make a homogeneous dough. Knead it 2 or 3 times with the heel of your hand to amalgamate it completely. Roll the pastry into a ball, wrap it in plastic wrap, and refrigerate until ready to use.

ganache barquettes with crème chantilly

These take time to make, but are worth the effort. Ideally you need 16 barquette molds, about 4³/4 inches long, 2 inches wide and ¹/2 inch deep, but 8 will do if you cook them in two batches. Cocoa butter and cocoa paste give the ganache a superior flavor and texture, but you can omit them and use extra chocolate. Leftover ganache can be shaped into small balls and rolled in cocoa to make truffles to serve with coffee.

Makes 8

7 ounces pâte sucrée (see left)
flour, for dusting
5¹/2 ounces best-quality bittersweet chocolate, or
dark couverture, melted
¹/2 cup sugar
16 unskinned almonds, dried in the oven
1 tablespoon peanut oil
4 marrons glacés (chestnuts in syrup)

Ganache:
3¹/2 ounces best-quality bittersweet chocolate, or
dark couverture, chopped (or 4¹/2 ounces, if
omitting cocoa butter and paste)
1³/4 ounces cocoa butter, chopped (optional)
1¹/2 tablespoons cocoa paste, chopped (optional)
6 tablespoons heavy cream
4 teaspoons liquid glucose or corn syrup
1 vanilla bean, split lengthwise

Crème Chantilly:
1²/3 cups heavy cream
1 vanilla bean, split lengthwise
4 tablespoons sugar syrup (page 188)

Roll out the pastry on a lightly floured work surface to a scant ⅛-inch thickness. Roll it around the rolling pin, then unroll it over 8 barquette molds. Break off a small piece of excess pastry, and use it to gently press the pastry into the shape of the molds. Roll the rolling pin across the top of the molds to cut off the excess pastry. Position an empty barquette mold inside each lined mold to act as a press (illustrated above) and refrigerate for 20 minutes.

Meanwhile, preheat the oven to 400°F. To make the ganache, put the chocolate into a bowl with the cocoa butter and cocoa paste, if using. Put the cream in a saucepan with the glucose. Scrape the vanilla seeds into the pan and heat gently. As soon as the mixture comes to a boil, pour the cream onto the chocolate mixture, stirring continuously with a wooden spoon until well amalgamated and smooth; do not overwork. Cover with plastic wrap and set aside.

Bake the pastry shells for 5 minutes, then remove the empty molds, and cook for another 2 to 3 minutes. Carefully unmold the pastry shells onto a wire rack and let cool. When cold, brush the insides with melted chocolate (see above), and set aside.

In a small pan, dissolve the sugar over a low heat, stirring, until it turns a pale caramel color. Immediately take off the heat and, using a fork, dip the almonds, one at a time, into the caramel to coat them all over. Place on a lightly oiled baking sheet.

To make the barquette "sails," fit a pastry bag with a plain tip about ¾-inch diameter. Fill with the ganache and pipe 8 sails onto a sheet of parchment paper (see below, left). Refrigerate for at least 1 hour, until hardened.

To make the crème Chantilly, put the cream in a bowl with the seeds from the vanilla bean and whip until it starts to thicken. Add the sugar syrup and beat until the cream leaves a trail when you lift the whisk.

To assemble, fit a pastry bag with a star tip, fill it with crème Chantilly, and pipe a generous plait into each pastry shell. Slide a palette knife under the chocolate sails, and arrange on the cream, pressing down lightly. Place a caramelized almond on either side of each sail, and half a marron glacé at one end.

caramelized melon and macaroon tart

This somewhat extravagant creation isn't a classic tart, but it brings together everything I love – crumbly pâte sucrée, soft macaroons, mouth-watering melon with a crunchy caramel coating, raspberries, and kirsch-flavored cream. You will need a 9-inch quiche ring, about ¾ inch deep.

Serves 8

10 ounces pâte sucrée (page 178)
flour, for dusting
2 *very small melons (grapefruit-sized)*
¹/₃ cup soft light brown sugar
2 *cups crème pâtissière (see right, about* ²/₃ *recipe)*
⁷/₈ cup heavy cream, whipped
2 tablespoons kirsch (optional)
25 *raspberries*
8 *tiny mint sprigs*
7 *soft macaroons (page 185), or ready-made macaroons*

Preheat the oven to 400°F. Lightly flour the work surface and roll out the pastry into a circle, about ⅛ inch thick. Roll the pastry onto the rolling pin, then unroll it onto the quiche ring so as not to pull it out of shape. Push it into the ring and pinch up the edges to flute them and raise them slightly above the edge of the ring. Slide onto a baking sheet and refrigerate for at least 20 minutes.

Prick the pastry base several times with a fork, then line it with baking parchment and fill with dried or ceramic baking beans. Bake in the hot oven for 25 minutes. Remove the baking beans and parchment, lower the oven temperature to 350°F, and bake for another 5 minutes, so that the pastry is well cooked. Transfer to a wire rack and let cool.

Meanwhile, prepare the melons. Cut off the skin, then cut each melon into 4 rounds, about 2 inches thick, discarding the ends. Scoop out the seeds from the center and place the melon rounds on a baking

sheet. Sprinkle with the sugar and wave a blow-torch over the surface to caramelize to a light golden color. To assemble the tart, place the pastry shell on a serving plate. Whisk the crème pâtissière thoroughly, then fold in the whipped cream and kirsch, if using. Pour this cream into the middle of the pastry case. It will subside slightly, but remain in a dome shape.

Put one melon round on the dome and arrange the other 7 melon slices around the cream. Place 4 raspberries in the hole in the central melon round; put 3 raspberries in each of the surrounding melon slices. Pop a sprig of mint into each cluster of raspberries. Finally, arrange the 7 macaroons around the edge. To enjoy the tart at its best, serve within an hour of assembling, before the caramel starts to melt.

crème pâtissière

I use this pastry cream in many desserts, including my caramelized melon tart (see left). You can keep it in the fridge for 3 or 4 days.

Makes about 3 cups

6 *egg yolks*
²/₃ cup sugar
¹/₃ cup flour, sifted
2 cups milk
1 *vanilla bean, split lengthwise*
pat of butter, or a little confectioners' sugar

Put the egg yolks in a bowl with a third of the sugar and whisk until the mixture is pale and has a light ribbon consistency. Add the flour and mix in carefully.

Put the milk and remaining sugar in a saucepan. Scrape the vanilla seeds into the pan and add the pod. Bring slowly to a boil, then pour a third onto the egg mixture, whisking continuously. Pour the mixture back into the pan and cook over a medium heat, stirring all the time. Bubble, stirring, for 2 minutes, then tip into a bowl. Remove the vanilla bean.

Dot flakes of butter over the surface or sprinkle lightly with confectioners' sugar to prevent a skin forming as the pastry cream cools.

choux pastry

This quantity of choux paste is enough to make 40 to 50 small buns, or profiteroles (see right). You can easily adapt the recipe to make savory choux. Omit the sugar and prepare the paste up to the point where the eggs have been incorporated, then add 1¼ cups finely grated Gruyère cheese. Shape and glaze with egg wash as for profiteroles, then dust with a little Gruyère and a touch of paprika before baking. Serve them barely warm, as an appetizer.

Makes about 1¾ pounds

½ cup water
½ cup milk
7 tablespoons butter, diced
½ teaspoon fine sea salt
1 teaspoon sugar
1¼ cups flour, sifted
4 eggs

Put the water, milk, butter, salt, and sugar in a medium heavy-based saucepan. Set over a high heat and bring to a boil. Cook for 1 minute, stirring continuously with a spatula.

Take the saucepan off the heat and quickly and evenly tip in the flour all at once, stirring vigorously all the time.

Still off the heat, stir the choux paste until it is smooth and well amalgamated.

Put the pan back on a low heat and stir for 1 minute to "dry out" the mixture slightly. Take care to avoid drying out the choux too much, or it will crack when you bake it. Tip the mixture into a bowl.

Immediately beat in two of the eggs, using the spatula to amalgamate them. Incorporate the other eggs, one at a time.

The paste should be smooth and glossy, and is now ready to use. If you don't want to use it immediately, brush the surface with a little beaten egg to prevent a skin or crust forming, which is liable to happen after a few hours.

profiteroles with passion fruit crème

These profiteroles are filled with crème pâtissière lightened with whipped cream and flavored with fragrant passion fruit. For a decadent dessert, dip them in chocolate sauce, or caramel if you prefer. Alternatively, you could simply fill the profiteroles with whipped cream or ice cream, and serve them the usual way – with chocolate sauce poured over.

Serves 8 to 10

1 quantity choux pastry (see left)
1 egg yolk mixed with 2 teaspoons milk (egg wash)

Filling:
2/3 cup heavy cream, whipped
1/2 quantity crème pâtissière (page 181), cooled
6 to 8 passion fruit, halved

To serve (optional):
1 quantity chocolate sauce (page 31)
confectioners' sugar, to dust

Preheat the oven to 400°F. Line two large baking sheets with baking parchment. Spoon the choux paste into a pastry bag fitted with a ⅝-inch plain tip and pipe small mounds in staggered rows onto the prepared baking sheet, spacing them well apart to allow room for the choux pastry to expand. (Staggering the rows helps the buns to cook evenly.)

Lightly brush the mounds with egg wash, then flatten them slightly with the back of a fork.

Bake the choux buns in the hot oven for 5 minutes, then open the oven door slightly, leaving it ajar about ½ inch to let the steam escape and allow the buns to crisp. Bake for another 10 to 15 minutes, depending on size, until golden brown. Transfer to a wire rack and let cool completely.

To make the filling, fold the whipped cream into the crème pâtissière. Scoop out the pulp and seeds from the passion fruit and fold into the mixture. Spoon into a pastry bag fitted with a small tip.

Assemble the profiteroles shortly before serving. Make a small hole in the side of each choux bun and pipe in the filling. If you wish, dip the tops into chocolate sauce to coat. Arrange the profiteroles on plates, allowing about five per serving, and dust with confectioners' sugar, if you like.

orange tuiles

These wonderful petits fours are so light and delicate that they explode in the mouth. I like to serve them with my coffee sabayon (page 31), but they complement almost all my desserts.

Makes about 20

1/2 cup plus 2 tablespoons sugar
1/3 cup flour
1/2 cup slivered almonds
3 1/2 tablespoons softened butter
grated zest of 1/2 orange
1/4 cup orange juice, strained

Preheat the oven to 350°F. Put the sugar, flour, almonds, butter, and orange zest in a bowl and beat well, then mix in the orange juice.

Take a scant tablespoonful of the mixture and push it off onto a nonstick or lightly buttered baking sheet. Repeat to use half of the mixture, spacing the heaps well apart to allow room for spreading. Dip a fork into cold water and use it to flatten the mixture, roughly into rounds. The more you flatten them, the thinner the tuiles will be, but the more fragile they will be to shape when cooked.

Bake in the oven for 4 to 5 minutes, until the tuiles have spread evenly and are a pale nutty brown color. Leave the tuiles on the baking sheet for 1 minute, then lift them off with a palette knife, and drape them around a rolling pin or a tuile mold so that they set into a curved shape.

When you have molded a few tuiles, you will need to return the baking sheet to the oven for 30 to 60 seconds, to soften the unshaped tuiles (which will have hardened on standing). Repeat to bake and shape the remaining mixture.

Keep the cooked tuiles in an airtight container until ready to serve.

cinnamon macaroons

These are excellent served with ice cream or sorbet, or simply with coffee. Like crèmes brulées, macaroons lend themselves to different flavorings; cinnamon is one of my favorites.

Makes about 30

1 2/3 cups confectioners' sugar
1 teaspoon ground cinnamon
3/4 cup toasted blanched almonds, ground, or
7/8 cup ready-ground
finely grated zest of 2 lemons, dried at room temperature for 2 to 3 hours
3 large or 4 medium egg whites (1/2 cup)
2 tablespoons sugar

Preheat the oven to 325°F. Sift the confectioners' sugar and cinnamon together into a bowl and mix in the ground almonds and lemon zest.

Beat the egg whites in another bowl until half-risen, add the sugar, and continue to beat until very smooth and firm. Scatter in the dry ingredients, delicately folding them in with a slotted spoon or spatula until perfectly amalgamated.

Line one or two baking sheets (depending on their size), with baking parchment. Put the mixture into a pastry bag fitted with a 1/2-inch plain tip and pipe out about 60 small balls, about 3/4-inch diameter, onto the baking sheets in staggered rows, spacing them well apart to allow room for spreading.

Bake in the oven for 5 minutes. The outside of the macaroons should be firm to the touch, but the inside should still be soft. Leave on the baking parchment for about 10 minutes, then detach the macaroons and sandwich them together in pairs, pressing delicately with your fingertips.

Pile the macaroons into a pyramid in a bowl, or serve them as petits fours. They are best eaten within 24 hours of baking, but if necessary, they will keep for a few days in an airtight container.

brioche

This large brioche is delicious for breakfast, served with jam or fruit compote. It will keep well in the larder for 2 or 3 days – simply warm it in the oven before serving.

Caramelized slices of brioche go beautifully with my poached apricots in assam tea syrup (page 111). Slice the brioche vertically through the "head" with a serrated knife, sprinkle the slices with confectioners' sugar, and broil until the sugar has melted into a glaze. This is when the gourmet becomes the gourmand!

You will need a brioche mold (preferably non-stick), that is about 8 inches across the top, 3½ inches across the base and 4 inches high.

Serves 10 to 12

2½ cups flour, plus extra for dusting
2 teaspoons fine salt
⅓ ounce compressed yeast (about ⅔ cake), or
1½ teaspoons active dry yeast
2½ tablespoons milk, at room temperature
4 eggs
½ pound (2 sticks) softened butter
1½ tablespoons sugar
1 egg yolk mixed with 1 tablespoon milk (egg wash)

Put the flour and salt in the bowl of an electric mixer fitted with the dough hook. Put the yeast and milk in a cup, whisk to dissolve the yeast, let it rise for a few minutes until it starts to foam, then pour the mixture onto the flour. Add the eggs, switch the mixer to low speed and knead until the dough is well amalgamated. Increase the speed a little and knead for 15 minutes, or until the dough becomes smooth and slightly elastic.

Meanwhile, cream the butter and sugar together in a bowl. Then, with the mixer still running, add to the dough, a little at a time. Continue to knead with the dough hook for another 15 minutes; by this time the dough will be glossy, smooth, and very elastic. Switch off the mixer and remove the dough hook.

Cover the bowl with a dish towel or baking sheet and leave in a warm place at about 80°F for about 2 hours, by which time the dough should have doubled in volume.

Deflate the dough by flipping it over 2 or 3 times with your fingers. Cover it again with the dish towel or baking sheet and place in the fridge for at least 6 hours, but not more than 24 hours.

To shape the brioche, put the dough on a lightly floured work surface and punch it down firmly a few times. Cut off one-third for the "head" and set aside. Shape the larger piece of dough into a ball and place it in the nonstick or lightly buttered brioche mold. Press two fingertips down into the center to make a hole in the "body."

Roll the smaller piece of dough into an elongated egg shape. Lightly flour your index and third fingers, place the more pointed end of the dough in the hole in the "body", and press it down into the center until it touches the base, running your floured fingers all round between the "body" of the brioche and the "head."

Lightly brush the brioche with egg wash and let it rise in a warm place for about 1½ hours. About 30 minutes before baking, preheat the oven to 400°F. Once the brioche has doubled in volume, lightly brush it again with egg wash. Dip the tips of scissors into cold water and snip evenly around the edges of the "body" in 8 places, dipping the scissors into the water before making each cut. Bake the brioche in the oven for 45 to 50 minutes.

Leave the brioche in the mold for 5 to 10 minutes, then unmold it and place on a wire rack.

pantry specials

chive oil

Makes 2 cups

2 cups olive oil
3/4 cup snipped chives
few drops of lemon juice

Flavored olive oils are the condiments of the moment. This chive oil will keep well for several days in a sealed bottle, so make plenty and use it to add flavor to grilled fish, crudités, or vinaigrettes. Adding a little lemon juice before serving reinforces the taste.

In a small saucepan, gently heat the olive oil to about 175°F. Drop in the chives, cover, and let cool for 1 hour. Whizz in a blender for 30 seconds, then strain the oil through a fine sieve into a bottle or jar.
Add a few drops of lemon juice to the flavored oil just before using.

orange oil

Makes 2 cups

2 cups olive oil
dried zests of 2 oranges
few drops of orange juice

Both this citrus oil and the chive oil (above) are delicious with cold lobster and langoustine salads. To dry orange zests, put them in a cool oven for a few hours; ready-dried zests are sold in jars.

Put the olive oil and dried orange zests in a container, seal tightly, and leave to macerate for at least 3 weeks. Strain the oil just before serving, and add a few drops of orange juice to boost the flavor, if necessary.

clarified butter

Melt the butter very gently and ladle the clear liquid through cheesecloth, leaving the milky deposit in the base of the pan.

sugar syrup

This is used for my Crème Chantilly, sorbets, and other desserts. To make 5½ cups, dissolve 3¾ cups sugar in 2⅔ cups water with 2 tablespoons liquid glucose or corn syrup, stirring occasionally, then bring to a boil. Boil for 3 minutes, skimming as necessary. Pour through a fine sieve, cool, and refrigerate for up to 2 weeks.

pickled baby beets

These are excellent with cold meats, smoked fish, and terrines.

Serves 8

24 small raw baby beets
1 1/4 cups white wine vinegar
1/4 cup soft brown sugar
1/4 cup granulated sugar
1 thyme sprig
1 bay leaf
salt and freshly ground pepper

Peel the beets, leaving on ¾ inch of the leaf stalks. Put in a saucepan, cover generously with cold water, season with salt and pepper, and bring to a boil. Lower the heat and simmer gently until tender; they will take at least 45 minutes. When you can insert a fine knife tip into the center without meeting resistance, the beets are cooked. Drain, refresh in cold water, and drain again.

Put the beets in a saucepan with all the other ingredients. Bring to a boil and boil for 1 minute. Take off the heat and set aside at room temperature for at least 24 hours. Refrigerate for up to 2 weeks.

pickled plums

Stephen Doherty kindly gave me this recipe. The damson plums are delicious with terrines and pâtés, cooked ham, and roast venison or pork, and add zing to sauces for game. Like all pickles, they develop character as they mature.

Makes 3½ pounds

2 1/4 pounds damsons, or other small tart plums, stalks removed
2 cups (1 pound) soft brown sugar
1 1/4 cups red wine
7/8 cup red wine vinegar
1 cinnamon stick
8 cloves
1 teaspoon coriander seeds
1 teaspoon allspice berries
2-inch piece fresh ginger, peeled and thinly sliced

Prick the damsons several times with a trussing needle or fine knife tip; set aside.
Put all the other ingredients in a saucepan, bring to a boil and boil for 5 minutes. Add the damsons and bring back to a boil. Immediately take the pan off the heat, cover with plastic wrap, and stand it on a rack. Let cool, then refrigerate for 12 hours.
Using a slotted spoon, transfer the damsons to sterilized preserving jars. Strain the liquid through a fine sieve into a pan and reduce by almost half to obtain a syrupy juice. Pour this hot juice over the damsons, seal the jars, and store in a dark cupboard for at least 1 month before use. Be sure to remind your guests to remove the pits.

acknowledgments

To my son Alain. We worked together for 20 days to produce the dishes for photography. The result was 200 step-by-step shots and 80 food photos ... not one of them needed a re-take. This is pure pride for a father!

Martin Brigdale. After six books together, I feel in such unison with Martin that I want to give the absolute best of myself, as this is what he demands of himself.

Kate Whiteman, who understands me so well that if I have missed something, her translation will cover my omission.

Mary Evans, for her artistic integrity, and her ability to push me that much farther in the most gentle way.

Janet Illsley, who overcame my hesitations of a new member of the side, to prove very quickly that she wanted to give the best of herself and be on a winning team.

Paul Welti, for excellent design work. His enthusiasm was infectious and at the end of a very long day's photography, I cherished the meal the team shared together, as Paul always wore a look of pure joy as he savored every mouthful.

Helen Trent, for superb photographic styling.

Claude Grant, my secretary and P.A., who gave up a significant chunk of her private time and family life to type and edit my French manuscript.

Robyn, my wife, who spread my vision beyond French cooking. As she applies her natural talent to preparing our daily communal meal, I hardly need venture beyond home to enjoy food from other ethnic origins.

specialist suppliers

CHOCOLATE, COUVERTURE,
COCOA BUTTER, ETC.

The Baker's Catalogue
P.O. Box 876
Norwich, Vermont 05055
Phone: 800-827-6836
Fax: 800-343-3002
www.kingarthurflour.com
Distributes Callebaut and other fine lines.

**New York Cake
& Baking Distributors, Inc.**
56 West 22nd Street
New York, NY 10010
Phone: 212-675-2253
Fax: 212-675-7099
Distributes Callebaut, Valrhona, and other fine lines.

Scharffen Berger Chocolate Maker, Inc.
914 Heinz Avenue
Berkeley, CA 94710
Phone: 510-981-4050
Fax: 510-981-4051
www.scharffenberger.com

GENERAL

Dean & Deluca
2526 East 36th Street North Circle
Wichita, KS 67219
Phone: 877-826-9246
Fax: 800-781-4050
www.deandeluca.com

SEAWEED AND SEA VEGETABLES
(also available at many health food stores and
organic markets)

Mendocino Sea Vegetable Company
P.O. Box 1265
Mendocino, CA 95460
Phone: 707-937-2050
www.seaweed.net

FISH FOR SASHIMI AND SUSHI
(note that it is best to have fresh fish
shipped only in the winter months)

Katagiri
224 East 59th St.
New York, NY 10022
Phone: 212-755-3566
Fax: 212-752-4197
www.katagiri.com

Wild Edibles
89 East 42nd St.
New York, NY 10017
Phone: 212-687-4255
Fax: 212-687-4477

index